POPULAR DEMOCRACY

POPULAR DEMOCRACY

The Paradox of Participation

GIANPAOLO BAIOCCHI
and
ERNESTO GANUZA

Stanford University Press
Stanford, California

Stanford University Press
Stanford, California

©2017 by the Board of Trustees of the Leland Stanford Junior University. All rights reserved.

Printed in the United States of America on acid-free, archival-quality paper

Library of Congress Cataloging-in-Publication Data

Names: Baiocchi, Gianpaolo, 1971– author. | Ganuza, Ernesto, author.
Title: Popular democracy : the paradox of participation / Gianpaolo Baiocchi and Ernesto Ganuza.
Description: Stanford, California : Stanford University Press, [2017] | Includes bibliographical references and index.
Identifiers: LCCN 2016036585 (print) | LCCN 2016037207 (ebook) | ISBN 9780804790611 (cloth : alk. paper) | ISBN 9781503600768 (pbk. : alk. paper) | ISBN 9781503600775 (ebook)
Subjects: LCSH: Political participation. | Democracy. | Municipal budgets—Citizen participation. | Municipal government—Citizen participation.
Classification: LCC JF799 .B34 2017 (print) | LCC JF799 (ebook) | DDC 321.8—dc23
LC record available at https://lccn.loc.gov/2016036585

Typeset by Classic Typography in 10.75/16 Adobe Garamond Pro

Contents

Acknowledgments

It is hard in a book like this, written about processes still unfolding, not to be taken in by current events. As we finish the book, political scenarios in Spain, the United States, and Brazil seem by turns dramatic, exciting, and uncertain. In Spain of course, Podemos, the new political-party-cum-movement, has in three years dramatically reshaped the political scenario after four decades of a staid, two-party deadlock that has been in place since the end of the Franco era. Whatever its electoral future or eventual policies, it will be impossible to speak of Spain without reference to this revolution against representation after the *indignados* movement in 2011. In the United States, Black Lives Matter has burst on to the scene, promising for some what appears to be the dawn of a new civil rights era. At the same time, right-wing vitriol and its angry electorate seem at a fever pitch in the country. And in Brazil, for many, the promises of participatory democracy, embodied by the perhaps crumbling Workers' Party, seem now in need of much greater scrutiny. The phrase "participation fatigue" seems to be more in the mouths of activists, scholars, and even international agencies today than even a few years ago.

We have been unable to follow the advice we routinely repeat to our students: pick an ending date for the research and stick to it. If you must, we usually advise, save more current happenings for an afterword. Instead, such events form a living backdrop to this book. It is our sincere hope that our dialogue with this context (and our acknowledgment of it) will help round out the historical arc we trace here, and rather than give the book a shortened shelf-life, make it more relevant to discussions we intend to interfere in. The book is also intensely personal and a reflection of our own trajectories in the worlds we describe. Though we have never thought of ourselves primarily as experts of participatory budgeting, we have both been involved with PB, in one way or another, for a decade and a half each. Between us, from our different vantage points, we have seen this world develop and radically change. While a reader might be forgiven for thinking this book is written from a disenchanted point of view, we try to leverage our stance for critical and productive purposes. Our disenchantment actually masks a deeper enchantment, not with participatory budgeting but with the utopia of "legislating the world to come."

We have accumulated friendships and debts in activist, practitioner, and scholarly worlds. We cannot hope to name them all, but some deserve special mention. Nicole Summers, who first worked on this project at Brown University, was a coauthor of Chapter 5 and generously agreed to including it in this book.

Brown University and the Watson Institute provided Gianpaolo an occasionally frustrating but exceedingly generative environment, in the form of very generously reduced teaching loads, ample research funds, and a lively intellectual community, to support his research and scholarship. The semester Ernesto spent there developing the ideas in this book was central to its genesis. Brown University summer research fellowships funded the excellent work of Donata Secondo and Nicole Summers for background research. The IGERT program at Brown also funded background research by Joshua Eubank. NYU and the Gallatin School, where the book was concluded, have provided a supportive and stimulating environment. NYU Global Initiatives provided Ernesto a productive visiting stint, while the NYU Gallatin Research Fellowship funded Grace Chen in research assistance.

Humanities Initiative at NYU also provided crucial translating funds for the final stage of the book, and some of the very important work of Nina Griecci in editing the English.

IESA in Córdoba continues to provide Ernesto a vibrant intellectual home, and the generous semester IESA supported Gianpaolo as a visiting scholar was also key to the development of this book. The Spanish Ministry of Economics offered a valuable grant (CSO2012-38942) to Ernesto to finish his own research.

Perhaps one of the single greatest debts we owe is to Kate Wahl, our indefatigable and unbelievably patient editor at Stanford University Press.

This book has emerged and evolved in conversation. While we cannot say if they would agree or disagree with the approach and findings of this book, the following colleagues and friends provided very important feedback on the manuscript, parts of it, the arguments, or even some of the ideas. Whether their feedback was of the supportive or the "stimulating counterpoint" variety, we are extremely thankful to Erik O. Wright, Michael Kennedy, David Kennedy, Patrick Heller, Nitsan Chorev, Cornel Ban, Keith Brown, Rich Snyder, Barbara Stallings, Peter Evans, Ananya Roy, Michael Burawoy, Gay Seidman, Richard Sennett, Gil Eyal, Iddo Tavory, Colin Jerolmack, Harvey Moltoch, Neil Gross, Francesca Polletta, Nina Eliasoph, Craig Calhoun, Claudio Benzecry, Ana Claudia Teixeira, Osmany Porto, Adrian Gurza Lavalle, Sonia Alvarez, Jeff Rubin, Millie Thayer, Agustin Lao Montes, Javier Auyero, Brian Wampler, Joan Font, Donatella Della Porta, Yves Sintomer, Caroline Lee, Ed Walker, Michael McQuarrie, Robert Fishman, Heloise Nez, Francisco Francés, Giovani Allegretti, Josh Lerner, Mike Menser, Ginny Browne, Rachel LaForest, Pam Jennings, Isaac Jabola-Carolous, Madeleine Pepe, and Marcelo K. Silva. We also owe a special gratitude to the next generation of scholars with whom we have debated these ideas: Diana Graizbord, Michael Rodriguez, Elizabeth Bennett, Alissa Cordner, Peter Klein, Stephanie Savell, Patricia

Garcia-Espin, Hillary Angelo, Daniel Aldana Cohen, Michelle Esther O'Brien, Brian Connor, Sinem Adar, and Sam Dinger.

Finally, our greatest debt is always personal.

Writing a book is always a struggle. This was a special one, as it was written by four hands across continents, time zones, and shifting professional commitments. It would have been literally impossible to finish the book without the presence of Hedwig Marzolf and Paula Chakravartty: their generosity and love are core pieces of the book. Their patience and wisdom were indispensable in our quest for coherence and the successful completion of the manuscript. Maybe they have heard a lot about participation, but we've learned a lot about love and patience.

Ernesto's boys—Adrian, Tasio, and Gael—have spent half of their lives with this book. They met Aisha and Safina, Gianpaolo's girls, at the halfway mark. The five push us every night to think about new imaginaries.

CHAPTER ONE

The Participation Age

Every day, participatory websites are created by parliaments, governments and local authorities, allowing citizens to contribute directly to decision-making processes, to debate political options in real-time, and thus to influence the decisions made by their representatives. Is this an answer to the so-called "crisis of politics" which manifests itself through citizens' disaffection from political parties and representative institutions?

—*Call for proposals for the SecondWorld Forum for Democracy, 2013*[1]

In November 2013 the Council of Europe organized the Second World Forum for Democracy in Strasbourg, France. More than 1,400 people from one hundred countries took part in this high-profile conference. The participants addressed twenty-one themes (organized in "labs") under the conference's overall theme, "Re-wiring Democracy: Connecting Institutions and Citizens in the Digital Age." The goal of the conference was for participants to collectively reflect on the challenges facing democracy in societies characterized by political disaffection and to consider how to address these challenges through online and offline participation.

One of the keynote speakers was Alderman Joe Moore, who four years earlier had set up the first experiment in participatory budgeting in the United States, in Chicago's 49th Ward. Less than two weeks after the conference, the Obama administration released its Second

Open Government Action Plan, which called for greater citizen involvement in government through democratic participation.[2] The document "recogniz[es] the value of the American public as a strategic partner" and outlines twenty-three specific initiatives to increase citizen participation and transparency. These include identifying and documenting best practices of participation, involving the public in agency rule making, increasing citizen science programs, and promoting community participation in budget decisions through tools like participatory budgeting.[3] At the time of the Open Government Action Plan's release, political leaders and experts from more than a dozen African countries were attending the International Conference on Citizen Participation in Tunis.[4] The organizers of this conference sought to encourage African citizens to participate in the management of public affairs across the continent.

Today participation is so ubiquitous that former U.S. secretary of state Hillary Clinton has described the current era as the "Participation Age." According to Clinton this era is marked by widespread expectation for voice and engagement, and "people whose voices were never heard [before] now can be heard."[5] Clinton is not alone in this assessment. As Matt Leighninger writes in his 2006 book *The Next Form of Democracy: How Expert Rule Is Giving Way to Shared Governance—And Why Politics Will Never Be the Same*, "In the 20th century, public life revolved around government; in the 21st century, it will center on citizens." Similarly very many others discuss the dawning of an era in which citizens have come to participate in all sorts of matters previously reserved for government bureaucrats and politicians. There is general agreement that we are living through what Caroline Lee, Michael McQuarrie, and Edward Walker have called a "participatory revolution." Today, they note, "across the political spectrum, increasing citizen voice is viewed as a necessary counterweight to elite power and bureaucratic rationality."[6]

Enthusiasm for citizen participation abounds, even if its magnitude is difficult to quantify. As Archon Fung suggests, part of the difficulty in estimating the extent of participation is that "the forms of participatory innovation are often local, sometimes temporary, and highly varied."[7] But all indications suggest it is a major trend. At the global level, the World Bank has invested $85 *billion* in development assistance for participation in the last decade.[8] For North America a survey from 2009 found that almost "all cities responded that they provided 'opportunities for civic engagement in community problem solving and decision making'" and that nearly three-fourths of them had instruments in place for citizen decision making in strategic planning that year.[9] In Western Europe the figures are similar, and several countries now mandate citizen participation as part of recent local government reforms.[10]

Whether citizen participation has *actually* displaced technocracy and elected politicians, a remarkable consensus has emerged around its desirability. Participatory democracy has become an imperative of our time, the subject of countless international conferences, government projects, and policy reforms, and is at the center of much recent contemporary political thinking.[11] In the last two decades an increasingly diverse cast of characters—multilateral donors, international NGOs, and policy experts alike—have touted "participation in government" as a panacea for a wide set of ills. Applied to both the Global South (particularly as seen in the "post-Washington consensus") and the Global North, participation has become a central tenet in thinking about government. Alongside ideas such as good governance, NGOs, civil society, grassroots action, decentralization, sustainability, local innovations, and social entrepreneurship, participation has now achieved the status of something unquestionably good and infinitely malleable. From the World Bank to Occupy and the Arab Spring, to new political parties like Podemos, to NGOs and consultancies, the idea of participation today occupies an exceptional position in the pantheon of policy prescriptions. Across the political spectrum and across policy domains it has become a privileged prescription for solving difficult problems and remedying the inherent flaws of democracy.

It has not always been this way. Up until the 1970s participatory democracy was largely associated with the political left, social movement idealists, or local cooperatives and generally viewed with suspicion by planners in mainstream institutions.[12] In the United States, for example, Francesca Polletta has documented participatory democracy's central role in the most important social movements of the 1960s and argued that participation conceived in this way was so important because it was *prefigurative*. The idea was that "to operate in radically democratic fashion was to prefigure the radically democratic society" and would thus "make the means reflect the ends."[13] Activists expected participation to bring about emancipation for citizens in a world otherwise dominated by political and economic elites.[14] And when the large movements went into eclipse as small-scale and local initiatives, sympathetic observers from the left, like Harry Boyte, imagined this was the beginning of "a backyard revolution" in which these prefigurative practices, premised on equality, solidarity, and social justice, would yield the transformative changes that movements themselves did not manage to achieve.[15]

However today we are witnessing a new political moment in which citizen participation is no longer the assumed domain of outsiders but has become widely encouraged, if not directly mandated, by governments and multilateral agencies. Corporations themselves are beginning to promote participatory processes as part of "corporate social responsibility" campaigns if not as part of efforts to neutralize negative publicity from grassroots campaigns against them, as Ed Walker has documented.[16] Participation is certainly no longer a counterpower; it has decisively become part of the planning of power itself. If talk of participation once evoked the "Port Huron Statement" and politically radical groups like Students for a Democratic Society, today we are as likely to hear it from the White House, British Petroleum, or the World Bank.

Moreover participation has evolved from being a corrective for entrenched professional expertise to being its own globalized field of expertise. According to Archon Fung the field of actors who "initiate and support citizen participation now constitute a diverse and mutually interacting" set of organizations and groups.[17] Among them in the United States, for example, are the "International Association for Public Participation, Everyday Democracy, the Kettering Foundation, and the Center for Deliberative Democracy at Stanford University" as well as "the National Coalition for Dialogue and Deliberation, the Participatory Budgeting Project, and the Deliberative Democracy Consortium."[18] Caroline Lee, who has studied the rise of the "Public Engagement Industry," dates its appearance to the late 1980s but notes a tremendous growth in the 2000s. Demand for services of the International Association for Public Participation, for example, tripled between 2005 and 2008.[19] Today participatory instruments quickly travel the world as processes of "fast policy transfer."[20] At times they seem to do so without apparent boundaries, as with the case we study in this book, which inverts the traditional journey of technologies from North to South.

The spread of participation globally—this "age of participation"—is profoundly paradoxical. In addition to its complicated origins and the broad cast of characters who today advocate it, the timing of events is also counterintuitive. Participation has spread precisely at the moment when an increasing number of decisions, because of their technical demands or their global scope, have become insulated from democratic decision making. Whether we are speaking of the specifics of global trade policy, the global property rights of water, environmental regulation, or the management of complex financial instruments, an increasing number of important decisions take place in juridical or expert settings completely beyond the reach of the demos.[21] More than one commentator has noted the coincidental rise of interest in participation and an increasing neoliberalization of public policy as well as an increase in inequalities.[22] Some have charged that participation not only has failed to arrest increasing inequalities but has directly been implemented to legitimate them. Colin Crouch has called the growing power of corporate interests and the concomitant emptying out of the power of democratic institutions to hold them accountable a growing postdemocratic condition.[23] Wendy Brown has described the current moment as a "neoliberal stealth revolution" that is systematically undermining the demos.[24] At the very least we are living in a context, as David Held and others have noted, of profound mismatch between scales of democracy and scales of decision making.[25]

Participation and Its Critics

This rise of enthusiasm for participatory democracy that has taken place around the world over the last twenty years has certainly inspired skepticism. Critical voices protest that while participatory democracy's scope has expanded, its emancipatory dimension has all but disappeared from policy discourse on the subject. Recently critics have disputed participatory boosterism for failing to address questions of power, inequality, and politics.[26] Frances Cleaver, for example, argues that the belief in participation is based on three postulates: "participation is intrinsically a 'good thing' (especially for the participants); a focus on 'getting the techniques right' is the principal way of ensuring the success of such approaches, and considerations of power and politics on the whole should be avoided as divisive and obstructive."[27]

More broadly, scholars have begun to point to participation, and participatory prescriptions specifically, as part and parcel of neoliberal reforms.[28] In general terms participatory democracy appears to have spread just as governments have retrenched. In many instances local governments have introduced participation to improve the fiscal management of public administrations facing financial constraints. Dwindling resources and uncertain futures have driven administrations to transform their practices to guarantee the services they promised. At the same time, they have had to satisfy new economic imperatives: efficiency, productivity, achieving goals, and so on. Is it any accident that, as some critics have charged, "participation is *the* buzzword of the neoliberal era?"[29]

Relatedly there is the worry that participation paves the way to a depoliticization of the public sphere, a point made most forcefully by scholars within the governmentality tradition. As part of a new rationality of government that calls forward an entrepreneurial citizen, participation emphasizes important characteristics of that citizen: self-regulation, responsibility for individual problems, and a nonconflictive partnership with the state.[30] In this formulation people are "conceived as individuals who are to be active in their own government."[31] Governmentality scholars' central concern is that participation works to deny the political basis of conflicts and inequities and shifts responsibilities for problems to individuals and communities.[32]

This last criticism is particularly poignant because governments under the philosophy of "new public management" in the 1980s and 1990s tried to emulate private enterprise by turning citizens into consumers of government services, as we describe in the next chapter. In that model, citizen participation served the role of identifying individual preferences. The public realm was thus reduced to a site of conflicts over individual preferences and to a channel of communication between service providers and clients rather than a space for collective self-determination.

While these critiques are useful, we believe scholars should not so readily dismiss these emerging forms of participatory democracy. Setting aside for a moment the question whether participation makes for effective public policy, we should be attentive to the possibility that participation may shift power relations in a given context. Participation implies a collective space and also presumes a certain equality between participants, with each person a partner in a shared world—of course "presupposing that one can play the same game as one's adversary."[33] In today's unequal and fragmented cities and societies it is a far from trivial accomplishment to establish settings for discussion premised on the equality of all participants and their common fate in the sense of public good. There is always something potentially subversive, and unpredictable, in arrangements that imply this equality.

Critics are also sometimes dismissive of the differences between the "new public management" of the 1980s and trends since the 2000s such as "public governance." New public management—with its idea of the citizen-consumer and its explicit goal of a minimal government modeled on the private sector—certainly sat more easily with neoliberal frameworks than current participatory frameworks, which do evoke both equality and a collective. Wendy Brown's account of the "neoliberal stealth revolution," for example, is one where all spheres of life are becoming subject to economic rationality, as "the demos disintegrates into bits of human capital; concerns with justice cede to the mandates of growth rates, credit ratings, and investment climates; [and] equality dissolves into market competition."[34]

In addition the spread of political participation around the world has not only been the prerogative of opportunist politicians or mega-agencies like the World Bank, nor is it *simply* an outgrowth of neoliberal thinking. In many if not most cases it is the result of the active work of NGOs and other organizations in partnership with reformers within the state. Today hundreds of civic organizations lobby for participation at the local, national, and international levels. A great number of specialists are trained in participatory practices, travel to other countries, and replicate participatory experiments. The specialists aim to widen democratic spheres and adapt the participatory instruments to local contexts. This global network in many ways resembles networks of "transnational advocacy," such as those fighting for human rights.[35] Looking at how participation templates travel complicates the perception of northern-based actors' dominance in generating those blueprints, as in the case of economic knowledge.[36] The story of the travel of participatory budgeting from Brazil to the Global North, as we describe later in the book, in some ways bears the mark of "counter-hegemonic globalization," to use the phrase of Peter Evans, insofar as it signals the belief that "transnational connections can potentially be harnessed to the construction of more equitable distributions of wealth and power."[37]

Finally we have to at least consider the possibility that participation may be the victim of its own success. In contrast to the past, participation today has jumped both the economic and the political efficiency hurdles. In the 1970s, for example, reports often criticized instances of participation for being little more than a disorganized crowd of people.[38] Today there are endless tools and techniques for managing participants and their expectations. These range from the field of "civic tech"—developing myriad technological devices—to many successful instances of in-person participation: participatory budgeting in Brazil, the debate over Iceland's constitution, and citizen juries in British Columbia, to name a few. Together these have shown that participatory democracy *can* be efficient and *can* manage large numbers of people within complex circumstances without creating any threat to the political order. Advocates argue that perhaps we have simply become good at participation, having now developed the tools and know-how to implement it across many settings. That the World Bank has become a proponent of participatory democracy at the global level may indicate that participation can infiltrate even institutions otherwise devoted to economic efficiency.[39]

The implementation of participation within these institutions could signify that participation is forcing those within these contexts to expand their horizons. In fact that is the strategic question that "real utopian" thinkers Archon Fung and Erik Wright force us to ask in their proposals for "empowered participatory governance."[40] Within the parameters of local governance in Europe and the United States—usually a site of retrenched governments—citizen participation could signal the broadening of the political subject, the acceptance of the other as colegislator in public affairs, and a subtle extension of the limits of democracy. While advocates acknowledge that participation may not always represent a transformational policy, it may nonetheless mark a step forward in democratic thinking and equality among the members of a political community.

Reframing the Question

The goal of this book is to offer a sustained reflection on this political moment. We do so with a specific purpose, which is less about accounting for these remarkable developments than asking about what they imply. To borrow James Ferguson's phrase, the point of the analysis here is to ultimately ask how this participatory revolution "may be transforming the field of political limits and possibilities."[41] It is an engaged book in that we have been part of the processes we describe and that our intention is very much to interfere in the terms of the debate.

But we are less concerned with whether participation is a "successful" policy or instrument than in how it comes to be assembled and what its effect may ultimately be in foreclosing some alternatives and opening others. The purpose of this book is not to settle the question whether e-voting is more or less effective than face-to-face deliberations at drawing out young or underprivileged participants. Our goal rather is to say something about what participation, as currently practiced, makes possible and what it might make possible. This book identifies the broader parameters of new governance—what we call the "new spirit of government"—and describes how one practice achieved the status of a global model in that framework. We then turn to an ethnographic account of the practice's landing in two very distinct contexts. Finally we revisit the lessons of those encounters and seek to make a strategic intervention into how they may serve an emancipatory project.

A word about our standpoint. As we alluded to above, the exponential rise of participation in the last two decades has fueled a debate between critics and boosters, and much like competing accounts of the rise of free markets, it pits opponents "that tell a formally similar story but with the moral polarity inverted."[42] Both critics and enthusiasts acknowledge an unprecedented growth of interest in and implementation of participation since the 2000s, but one set of analysts sees it as a pervasive and more perverse form of neoliberal responsibilization while another marks it as a citizen revolution. We very much take up the challenge that Ferguson has laid down for scholars to "engage with these new configurations of governmental power in a way that goes beyond the politics of denunciation, the politics of the 'anti.'"[43] This implies both forgoing "the pleasures of the easy, dismissive critique" and attention to "the rich world of actual social and political practice, the world of tap-turning and experimentation."[44] Fundamentally if advocates of participation are guilty of turning a blind eye to power, and politics, and interests, then critics often ignore its potential as a space of possibilities. Those limits and possibilities, we believe, are to be found in the world of specific practices and contexts, not in general logics.

The study in this book is somewhat unusual. In the years that it took to put it together we have relied on observations, interviews, analysis of texts, and devices, as well as much reflection and conversation about our own involvement in this world. Doing so has upended our own understandings of what anthropologist David Mosse has described as the division between "desk" and "field" in ethnographic work.[45] It is more common in the world of participation today for engaged scholars to cross boundaries into the world of practice and implementation than for those in the world of practice to step back and offer a more distanced analysis.[46]

We understand this book as an ethnographic account in the sense of understanding meanings, practices, and relationships, yet it is more of an ethnography of following actors than observing sustained inter-action at any one place or with one set of actors.[47] We build on the work of previous ethnographers who have sought to capture objects in motion across global landscapes.[48] And we draw on recent criti-cal urban studies from geographers who have called attention to "the critical investigation of policies-in-motion across multiple sites, with a focus on how regulatory practices and institutions achieve 'model' sta-tus, and circulate and mutate between places and through distended policy networks."[49]

We are also fundamentally inspired by the call from Science and Technology Studies who insist on studying process *in the making*, "be-fore the controversies involved in its fabrication are closed, before the complexities of its inner working are taken-for-granted" and before "the patterns of organizational power and influence [. . .] are forgot-ten or rationalized."[50] In doing so we follow the story from contro-versy to controversy, from one city in Brazil in the late 1980s through to Europe and then the United States in the 2010s. In an important sense our approach is also indebted to microhistory and its insistence on reconstruction of larger realities from smaller events.[51]

In this context our framework also benefits a great deal from what Jamie Peck has described as an emergent "comparative imagination" that "has constructively opened the horizon for a different kind of urban studies" beyond comparisons structured around nation-states or even the idea of precisely comparable units.[52] Accordingly, in seek-ing to understand participatory experiments both in a wider field of thinking about governance and in very specific contexts, we have heeded the warning to avoid "unreflexive and shorthand uses of 'neo-liberalism' as an all-purpose, ambient signifier, ready for standardized application irrespective of context."[53]

The Research Literature and Its Limits

Our approach here is different from much of the current scholarship that approaches participatory democracy empirically. By now an abundance of literature has emerged alongside the growth of these participatory endeavors. Much of this scholarship implicitly adopts the point of view of those implementing participatory experiments, if it is not directly carried out by those implementers or their allies themselves. That is, scholars often ask questions that mirror those of the projects' implementers or its funders, such as: Who participates? What is the depth and scope of participation? Is the project successful? Is the process actually participant centered and does it take the view of participants?

As useful as that literature has been and as much as we rely on its specific insights for the arguments we make here, we purposefully depart from it. We do so for several reasons. First, the literature generally takes for granted the democratizing effects of participation. It is not uncommon for scholarship to take the participation of several thousand participants in some process as prima facie evidence of democratization or empowerment. Similarly scholars assume that stating agreement to "democratic values" or "trust in government" in response to questions pertaining to participation is evidence of democratization. The literature very seldom asks if participation extends beyond the institutionalized forum and almost never addresses the fundamental question of how preferences are aggregated and translated into actual outcomes in participation.[54]

Second, the literature nearly always privileges the *local forum* as the central unit of transformation. Participant surveys or ethnographies take the meeting as the center of social action and the remaining institutional apparatus fades from view. In fact scholars pay attention to the processes as a participant might, focusing on the quality of deliberation and debate. These scholars often view government machinery as ambiguous or peripheral to the process.[55] The literature seldom shines a light on the processes of implementing participatory instruments themselves or the conflicts these efforts generate within administrations. This localist reading thus excludes any consideration of democratic innovations beyond the procedures to which they are normally applied and, more importantly, hinders discussions of their capacity to transform existing power relations. Mark Purcell has described this as the "local trap" into which analysts can easily fall.[56] And Jamie Peck correctly warns that "'alternatives' too should be evaluated in and against these wider fields of difference, not as separatist enclaves."[57] Although in this book we sometimes cover seemingly micro details of particular experiences, we go to some pains to locate these in the broader context of governance, power, and politics and also in the context of broader changes in thinking about governance.

Most crucial for us however is that the literature takes for granted how administrations, practitioners, and participants assemble "participation." That is, before asking what participation *does*, scholars rarely ask what participation *is* and what it means within specific sites. While the literature covering this topic is insightful, it is often unvariegated and relies on retrospective accounts of "a series of inevitable stages moving from the abstract to the concrete."[58] Both critics and proponents of participation tend to overlook how any participatory project requires allies, and how any such project provokes tensions and conflicts. Whether scholars describe it a priori as a neoliberal project or celebrate it as a prima facie democratic advance, participation in either case seems to arrive on the scene as ready-made and is then tested for its effects.

We look instead to the insights of the more dispassionate, usually comparative projects that have looked at various local contexts, meanings, and politics of participation. Scholars such as Gabriel Hetland, Benjamin Goldfrank, Brian Wampler, Stephanie McNulty, Yves Sintomer, and Joan Font, among others, have long insisted that participation not be looked at outside of broader political contexts.[59]

The institutionalization of participation is always "a *collective* process" in which heterogeneous actors come together around issues and agree to work on them jointly.[60] Critics of participation-as-neoliberalism downplay the collective nature of participation projects. Participatory projects are never the work of a single omnipotent and authoritative actor. These projects usually involve a range of participants from different levels of government—"stakeholders," broadly defined—and a wide range of experts. Then there is the work of enrolling additional actors to participate. With each new actor enrolled there is always some redefinition of what participation will consist of. On the other hand, those who celebrate participation often underemphasize the power dynamics and conflict that are inherently part of establishing participation. The very definition of participation—the project's goals or who can be a legitimate participant—represents the power of some agents to define those agendas. As we discuss later in the book and as any insider to participatory processes can attest, participation also calls forth laborious efforts by the organizations of government to mobilize resources, allies, and agents with the aims of fixing its limits, of defining a proper field of operations, and of neutralizing runaway participatory arguments.

In shifting the conversation away from the point of view of participation's implementers, we are calling for a critical distance and a sense of estrangement from these processes. We have come to believe that greater agnosticism would benefit critical scholars evaluating participatory processes, rather than relying on what anthropologists call "ontological complicity."

Democratization from Above

Taking our cues from Pierre Lascoumes and Patrick Le Gales, for us participation is an *instrument,* a "device that is both technical and social, that organizes specific social relations between the state and those it is addressed to, according to the representations and meanings it carries,"[61] which implies that participatory instruments do not arrive ready-made.[62] Moreover when these projects do "land," they represent an array of actors with different interests invested in (or opposed to) the device. Policy instruments in this way "are not neutral devices: they produce specific effects, independently of the objective pursued (the aims ascribed to them), which structure public policy according to their own logic."[63] Here we suggest that new participatory devices (democratic innovations) open a new political context with important effects on democratic performance.

Nearly all democratic innovations today are developed around the idea of everyone's equal right to be heard—that is, participants are invited to decide conjointly and there are no political hierarchies in the decision-making process. It does not mean that all democratic innovations are successful stories of enabling broad participation, but rather that democratic performances are going to be structured from that idea. For that reason these efforts imply a universal framework of political action, which aims to achieve a collective understanding from which all kind of actors will justify or critique the flow of events. This encourages, at least inside the participatory process, the emergence of a common space around which politics can revolve. From such a space the conflicts of power that arise through democratic innovations reveal the struggle for sovereignty. Debate between citizens, political representatives, and technical experts depends on the concept of political equality, which allows the participant to assert herself as a partner in a shared world, moving politics onto the terrain of mutual empowerment.

Throughout the book we focus on the question of *political co-ordination*. For us political coordination is the answer to the central problem in democracies: How are different identities, claims, and interests in a complex society constructed and coordinated? Under what principles are they rendered equivalent? What is the limit of the demos, and what is its reach? Sociologists and social theorists from Max Weber to Jürgen Habermas and Charles Tilly, who considered conditions under which diverse societal demands are debated and met, have treated these as central questions. In very broad terms, these are the concerns of relational political sociologists. And recent critical theorists have also taken up these concerns. Ernesto Laclau, for example, is concerned with the logic of equivalence between different demands and between actors in complex societies,[64] while Bruno Latour insists that we investigate, first of all, how the demos is assembled. Jacques Rancière asks principally who is allowed to participate in decision making and in the division of societal rewards, and what kinds of identities and claims are considered sensible.[65]

Attentiveness to political coordination implies attention to *justifications*. In societies where there is some room for the interpretation of the social and political order, the question of why this policy and not another also remains open and is fraught with ambiguities. But our focus here is on specific effects rather than general principles at play. Political coordination takes place through specific instruments (democratic innovations) that have specific effects in structuring political interactions according to their own logic. In this case it is the logic of making decisions without hierarchies.

From this point of view democratic innovations pose a number of questions. They may pose important challenges to democratic performance, awakening resistance and criticism from within administrative apparatuses, as we'll see. Unlike traditional political thinking on the left, the concept of participation through democratic innovations reconciles protests and proposals. Participation begins not from a place of conflict but from one of shared interest. The participant listens to what others say and then decides what is best. Even without recourse to the notion that there may be no good citizens, the participant is transposed to a place in which she must make collective decisions and where a diversity of strategies might be deployed. Yet the open stage of democratic innovations is already enclosed within the boundaries of the debate, which in the majority of cases are imposed by those in government. Similarly "equality" is an automatic assumption that may mask structural difficulties preventing some voices from being heard. Finally it is not clear what is under discussion or how it should be discussed. For example, can everybody in fact participate in the debate? The "problem space" defined by these democratic innovations provokes core questions: What is to be decided? Who decides what is up for debate? How will decisions be made? Furthermore what kind of political project do these processes represent (is it more democratic or less?).

In the following chapters we will analyze the democratic innovations at this juncture. In the next chapter we look at these participatory institutions in more detail, discussing the principles of political coordination that orient them. We recognize that these processes are closely linked to globalization. Democratic innovations travel fast, are replicated, copied, and easily adapted in widely differing contexts. In that sense their proliferation around the world in recent years offers us an ideal framework with which to interpret globalization. Why do these processes take place, and does their participatory nature produce certain consequences? Chapter 3 is thus devoted to analyzing how democratic innovations travel and the kind of influence the travel itself has on specific instruments. In the succeeding chapters, 4 and 5, we will look more deeply into the aforementioned issues regarding the limits of democratic innovations, using ethnographic work carried out in the United States and Spain. Chapters 3, 4, and 5 take as their specific example the inception and development of a particular democratic innovation—participatory budgeting—in three different cities: Porto Alegre (Brazil), Chicago (USA), and Córdoba (Spain). Participatory budgeting is a democratic innovation based on the simple premise that ordinary citizens should have a say in how public budgets are decided. Developed among leftist social movements and municipal administrators in Brazil in the late 1980s, it has since been copied and adapted in hundreds of municipalities around the world.

Participatory budgeting is one of the marquee participatory institutions of the contemporary moment, routinely being included in lists of best practices in both the Global North and Global South. It thus provides a strategic angle from which to address the fundamental questions the current era asks of us—questions which critics and promoters alike have increasingly asked: What does this turn to participation mean? Is it transformative? Is it a "quiet revolution," as some enthusiasts have argued? Are these social changes that lie at the interstices of power, or simply neoliberalism in disguise? Fundamentally can we still think in terms of social transformation? The questions are broad and our answers are modest, but we hope these chapters will contribute to the current debate on democracy. In the final chapter we offer some reflections from a wider political perspective on the direction in which our analysis might lead.

CHAPTER TWO

The New Spirit of Government

The electoral victory of Bill de Blasio as mayor of New York City was in many ways unprecedented. Arriving as he did with a history of leftist activism and powerful electoral rhetoric around the "two cities of New York" of the haves and the have-nots, he explicitly invoked the language of the "99%" from 2011's Occupy movement. Mayor de Blasio's victory represented the triumph of the "other New York," the one left behind by years of economic growth and growing inequality under previous administrations. His victory also represented a symbolic but powerful break with the self-styled "CEO-mayor" Michael Bloomberg, who had brought business-world ideas and reforms to New York City Hall for eight years, including a highly technocratic orientation.[1] If Bloomberg had been known for emphasizing the "citizen-as-consumer," public-private partnerships, and economic development, de Blasio promised dialog with citizens, inclusiveness, and social justice.

In New York City the months between the election and inauguration are typically a period of high anticipation as the mayor-elect announces cabinets and policy directives. Historically during this time closed-door negotiations have taken place between representatives of powerful interests. However, following de Blasio's election, civic groups active in the city promised a more inclusive process. Ten large organizations under the leadership of the Open Society Foundation put together a two-week event, Talking Transition, to allow

New Yorkers "to make their voices heard on a range of issues such as police practices, education, and drug policy." This event marked the city's "first open transition."[2] According to Christopher Stone, one of the architects of Talking Transition, the idea was to introduce citizen voices to the political process and break with the tradition in which "the think tanks take over" after an electoral campaign's results are announced.[3]

From November 9 to November 23 a temporary, five-thousand-square-foot enclosed tent was erected in Tribeca in lower Manhattan. The tent had a transparent covering to evoke openness. Inside was a large open conference space, a video booth to record messages to mayor-elect de Blasio, workspaces with iPads for answering surveys, a low-tech suggestion box, and spaces for stickers with written ideas for the new administration. In addition the event dispatched some one hundred multilingual canvassers and set up three mobile kiosks at the city's libraries and busy intersections to gather information.[4] And in what was described as a "great participatory policy-making conference,"[5] over the two weeks dozens of community, nonprofit, and policy advocacy groups presented ideas for the new administration. Topics included school reform, environmental improvements, affordable housing, and proposals to improve transparency and civic engagement.

The event ended on a Saturday afternoon with a "facilitated town hall-style discussion" of city residents' thoughts on "the highest priorities for the new mayor."[6] Mayor-elect de Blasio visited the event several times and praised its success: "I'm thrilled that so many people are participating and I think there's going to be a lot of hidden gems in this process."[7] In the end, according to organizers, some *fifty thousand* New Yorkers attended Talking Transition and many more submitted input through other means. The process was a success and according to Stone, "The next question is, *Will the ideas and insights work their way into government?* Only the future will tell."[8]

Talking Transition is emblematic of new forms of participation. It is open and inclusive, and places "ordinary citizens" at the center. Participation is not mediated by what are described as representatives of "the old ways," like unions, social movements, or political parties. And participation is not supposed to be conflictive, as it promises a win–win for all: governments get better input, citizens are heard, new solutions are dreamed up, and a more encompassing and inclusive sense of the common good emerges out of deliberation for all involved. "Potential benefits," writes Taewoo Nam, "include enhanced engagement with citizens, improving the citizen-government relationship, and facilitating policy implementation."

This kind of engagement, Nam goes on, "is about political empowerment, a new channel of self-expression, better realization of individual and community values, and a democratic pursuit of one's beliefs and goals."[9] This new thinking accepts the individual, private life, and a plural society but recasts the common sphere as a problem-solving site that involves everybody in decision making, rather than as a space of struggle. In the end, advocates argue, governance is improved and citizens are brought closer and closer to the workings of government itself while realizing their own individual and community goals, fighting the powerful sense of alienation, apathy, and disaffection.

Yet participatory processes like Talking Transition are fundamentally more bounded than a word like *empowerment* would suggest. They are bounded in their *form*, as they exclude conflict and protest, in their *goals* of improving governance, and by the fact that *terms* are set from the start by those promoting the participation. Because existing administrations are the main implementers of these new arrangements, they hold the power to set the limits of the conversation—they decide the topics of debate and the terms of discussion. Generally speaking, participants are asked to answer a set of questions decided by those who are implementing participation, questions deeply conditioned by their sense of what is possible, desirable, or feasible. For us these democratic innovations evoke the more general contradictory character of contemporary democracies that operate on the principle of what philosopher Jacques Rancière has called the "partition of the sensible." Better and more just distributions are possible and desirable but, the worry goes, the question of just *what* is "sensible" is pushed aside.[10]

Unlike previous eras when citizen participation was associated with social movements or projects for social transformation, it now takes place within the "new spirit of government." This chapter traces the origins of these new participatory instruments and discusses several specific instances that have been taken up in the United States and Europe. Practitioners and academics have celebrated citizen participation as a solution to the problem of political disaffection, which threatens to break the bond between citizen and government. Receptive governments constantly innovate and experiment with the participatory templates in circulation, as new consultants and experts provide a growing assortment of ways with which to facilitate citizen communication.

When we speak of a new spirit of government we are referring to a new normative framework guiding thinking about governance. In this new framework, activating the citizenry through democratic participation has become a central objective of government intervention. Public participation has become a global instrument today that is to be used against the destabilizing tendencies within representative democracy itself, guaranteeing governments greater legitimacy and an alternative means of addressing the social demands that threaten governability. Democratic innovations promote a political project that differs from the laissez-faire endeavors of the 1980s and the reinvention, under "new public management," of how governments function. Under new public management, governments and local administrations addressed the problem of disaffection by incorporating business practices that regarded citizens as individual consumers. In contrast, today the emphasis has shifted to practical public participation and a search for optimal outcomes, often through the use of technical instruments. This position, though at odds with new public management thinking, is not anchored in a traditional leftist vision of a counter-hegemonic project either. A counter-hegemonic project would seek to create participatory institutions as spaces of conflicting interests and consolidate power from below. Participatory institutions today are instead based on a propositional logic that pushes aside the dynamic of demand and protest.[11]

To fully make sense of the seeming contradictions of the new spirit of government, it is necessary to more precisely locate how and when participation emerges as what anthropologist David Scott has called a "problem-space," that is, "an ensemble of questions and answers around which a horizon of identifiable stakes (conceptual as well as political-ideological stakes) hangs."[12] Identifying a problem-space means distinguishing the contours of debate and intervention, determining legitimate questions, and exploring the broader "context of rival views."[13]

Our approach here of course owes to the magisterial efforts of sociologists Luc Boltanski and Ève Chiapello, who first identified the "new spirit of capitalism" that has emerged in Europe since the 1970s. In order to analyze changes within capitalism, they focus on prescriptive managerial texts that inform managers "of the latest developments."[14] We similarly trace the appearance of participation as a problem while also sketching broader changes in thinking about government itself, beginning with the idea of a democracy in crisis in the 1970s through to the appearance of "new public management" in the 1970s and the emergence of "public governance" in the early 2000s.

The Many Crises of Democracy

Citizen participation appeared as a serious issue for governments in Europe and North America in the 1970s, having nearly disappeared in the earlier part of the twentieth century under the hegemony of procedural definitions of democracy.[15] The landmark 1975 study *The Crisis of Democracy* marks participatory democracy's definite return to mainstream policy debates. Authored by Michel Crozier, Samuel P. Huntington, and Joji Watanuki, this influential text, originally written as a report for the Trilateral Commission, studied the disaffection in European, American, and Japanese democracies. The study argued that governments in industrialized nations faced a lack of legitimacy and serious threats to their ability to govern as a result of the excesses of the 1960s. In Europe, the report argued, governments were "overloaded with participants and demands," while in the United States the impulse was to simultaneously "make government less powerful and more active." As Huntington put it, "the vitality of democracy in the United States in the 1960s produced a substantial increase in governmental activity and a substantial decrease in governmental authority." Under the unsettling header of "the crisis of democracy," specialists and organizations dedicated increasing amounts of time and resources to the problem of the democratic link between political leaders and citizens. Questions always pointed in the same direction: What degree of political participation could or should be acceptable in modern democracies?[16]

The framework of *The Crisis of Democracy* (which continues to be influential today) set out in broad terms the problem of the relationship between governments and their citizens in democratic polities. The authors noted four problems: (1) the reduced legitimacy of political leadership experienced at the beginning of the 1970s; (2) the excessive growth in the demands made by society arising from social upheaval, which risked overloading the work of government; (3) the intensification of political competition and the possible drift toward populist governments or excessively fragmented political landscapes; and finally, (4) the emergence of new forms of political participation inherited from the protests of the late 1960s, which according to the authors threatened the stability of representative institutions.

For the authors of *The Crisis of Democracy* industrialized countries clearly faced an "excess of democracy." They saw the political disaffection of the mid-1970s as an immediate reaction to the convulsive 1960s. Social movements in Paris and Berkeley had put openness, freedom, and bottom-up democracy on the agenda, threatening the foundations of procedural democracy.[17] Among the principal targets of these changes were centralized bureaucracies, seen as both inefficient and removed from average citizens.

Civic participation held a significant place within the new social relationships emerging across Europe and the United States in the late 1960s; consequently there were many efforts to channel the demands of movements into forms of participation. To many academic specialists like the authors of *The Crisis of Democracy* this desire to participate was more likely to lead to disorder than anything else. Many of the participatory experiments of the 1960s and 1970s, emerging as they did from social movements, were routinely labeled *destabilizing*, and provoked the use of very tight controls over the new forms of participation.

While the pendulum of the discussion would eventually swing so that forty years later participation would be encouraged, the terms of the discussion would remain essentially the same. All discussions of participation since have revolved around the problem of political disaffection, because scholars consider the apathy of the public a medium- and long-term systemic risk.[18] Experts argued that governments without democratic legitimacy would be exposed to electoral turbulence and would lack the support necessary to make strategic decisions. The increasing demands facing governments and the difficulty of prioritizing these demands in absence of legitimate procedures would eventually render states ungovernable.[19] The end result might be "bad governments"—either populist or fragmented.

In the decades since *The Crisis of Democracy* the policy prescriptions to address this problem have changed. In recent years international organizations like the United Nations Development Programme (UNDP), the Organisation for Economic Co-operation and Development (OECD), and the World Bank have repeatedly asserted the importance of halting this decline, in the majority of cases through participatory reforms to bring citizens closer to government. In this way political disaffection has become a yardstick by which to measure the development of participatory politics: the greater the disaffection, the more advisable participation becomes.[20]

To fully make sense of these changes between the 1975 report and events like New York City's Talking Transition, it is important to keep in mind the sea changes in thinking about government that took place after the fiscal crises of the 1970s, which manifested in the form of the business-inflected philosophy called new public management.

From Bureaucracy to the Market: Rise of New Public Management

Most scholars date the emergence of "new public management" to the late 1970s and early 1980s in Britain. However, the label did not come into common usage until much later when Christopher Hood, a professor of government at Oxford, formalized and put it to use.[21] Public *management* overtook older ideas of public *administration*. New public management (NPM) is a proposal to streamline and improve government by focusing on "three Ms": markets, managers, and measurement.[22] NPM split large bureaucracies into smaller, fragmented units, fostering competition between different public agencies, and between public agencies and private firms, and incentivizing government efficiency along economic lines.[23] The OECD defines it as decentralization, management by objectives, contracting out, competition within government, and consumer orientation.[24] New public management has led to a durable and extremely influential set of reforms, which overtook earlier ideas of progressive administration with its "highly distinct public sector."[25]

This was of course more of a gradual transformation than a radical one. Many Western countries had achieved notable levels of success (France's Thirty Glorious Years or the post–World War II prosperity in the United States), which took place around two interrelated axes: the economy and the political imaginary. We have already mentioned the culture of protest that spread around the world after the 1960s, without which the reconfiguration of government would have been unthinkable. It became increasingly difficult in the public's mind to conceive of a closed administration that implemented programs from the top down, showed no interest in citizen involvement, and presented itself to the public as working in the general interest and for the common good.[26]

Crucially, new public management sought to capture a part of the political imaginary of the 1960s. Community activists were repelled by the long shadow of the bureaucrat, whose imprint was seen in impersonal and top-down public projects. The near-mythical battle in the 1960s between Jane Jacobs and Robert Moses over the fate of Greenwich Village in New York City captured these sentiments. Jacobs, a mother, journalist, and untrained urban planner, led a series of community protests for nearly a decade against the seemingly unstoppable Moses, New York City's master monument and highway builder, over his plans for an expressway that would displace the neighborhood. Jacobs's victory seemed to strike a blow on behalf of local communities and the average citizen and against centralized planning, technical experts, and political elites.[27]

New public management sought to capture this sentiment, with its ideal of matching its objectives to the needs of the citizens, and managed to draw the old administration out of its closeted mind-set and link it to the public. That Moses had built 150,000 units of public housing in his tenure while Jacobs's arguments could be mobilized on behalf of a laissez-faire minimal state made the match even easier. The stifling and redistributive state was seen as the enemy of creativity, innovation, and community. New public management would also separate politics from policy. Thus, in order to respond to the challenges of the time, NPM promoters organized agencies to be as efficient and as close to the citizenry as possible.[28]

Not until the economic crisis of the 1970s though did those in government begin to drive the transformation of public administration. Government officials established a new equilibrium between the government and the governed, partially taking up the new political imaginary of NPM. Prior to the 1970s, reigning Keynesian economic ideas provided a set of postulates for urban governance. The Keynesian city, writes David Harvey, had its "social, economic, and political life organized around the theme of state-backed, debt-financed consumption."[29] Under nationally driven plans and in a context of strict regulation of competition between cities and regions, cities became sites of large infrastructure investments. Yet as the global economic crisis hit in the mid-1970s, municipalities most acutely felt the fiscal shortage. New York City notoriously came near bankruptcy in the mid-1970s, and by the early 1980s municipal governments were in dire straits throughout the United States and Europe.[30] The conservative revolutions driven forward by the British and American governments throughout those same decades aggressively dismantled what were seen as oversized and overprotected government institutions. The reforms instead promoted lean, decentralized, competitive, and entrepreneurial minimal states.[31]

The dismantling of the welfare state and the hollowing out of state institutions are well documented, but it is only recently that scholars started to pay sustained attention to the concurrence of participatory institutions at the time.[32] In the 1970s and 1980s many municipal authorities adopted participatory structures, the majority of which were based on some version of citizen advisory boards. Scholars who have examined these participatory boards found them to be minimally participatory, with very limited impact on political decisions and democratization processes.[33] Nonetheless this proliferation of experiments in participatory politics in the United States and Europe signified the first break from the old form of administration insofar as the public's involvement in managing government affairs began to constitute part of the administrative architecture. This rupture situated the public within the parameters of business, which generated a renewed role for technocrats and professionals within government, causing many observers to question the headway made by democratic participation. Indeed, new public management encouraged citizen passivity toward the management of public affairs; yet unlike the older form of administration it recognized that government was subject to public influence, albeit through indirect avenues.[34]

The fact that these new modes of government appeared during a time of crisis cast a shadow over these institutions. The economic crisis of the 1970s caused a significant reduction in public expenditure and a shift of governmental responsibilities to municipal levels, which local politicians combined with civic participation efforts. This was the moment when, in Europe, local governments implemented the first participatory structures and, in the United States, federal administrations encouraged community development corporations (CDCs).[35] Conceived of as small participatory institutions, nearly always in low-income neighborhoods, CDCs promoted the economic integration of local residents through the creation of businesses and jobs. Critics of the time charged that CDCs substituted redistribution and equality with participatory decision making. With no ambition for social change the CDCs offered charity and economic integration rather than political participation or empowerment. Critics have also associated CDCs with the "hollowing out" of government and the transfer of responsibilities downward to cities.[36] For example, in the 1980s federal aid to cities fell by 60 percent while the number of CDCs rose from one hundred to two thousand. Although the transfer of responsibilities to cities gave them a greater role, it did so in the context of increasing austerity. More and more, cities were asked to manage financial deficits while becoming responsible for a greater share of service provision. Thus participatory processes of the time, like CDCs, were criticized for providing cover for increasing austerity.[37]

If the appearance of new public management is usually associated with the conservative policies of Margaret Thatcher in 1970s England, it reached its zenith in the early 1990s across the Atlantic with the election of Bill Clinton, a Southern liberal Democrat, to the presidency of the United States. Clinton represented a new kind of Democrat who believed in cutting back government. His campaign slogan, to "reinvent government," came from the title of an NPM book published just in time for the 1992 election. That book, subtitled *How the Entrepreneurial Spirit Is Transforming the Public Sector*,[38] promised new ways to import business-sector efficiency techniques to streamline government and make it more results oriented. In 1993 the White House led the National Performance Review process, which resulted in the reduction of over 400,000 federal jobs. According to recollections from the time, laminated cards were handed out to federal employees with the four principles of reinventing government, the first of which was "Putting customers (the American taxpayers) first."[39] The National Performance Review was one of the most ambitious administrative reforms in recent history in size or scope.[40] Its mantra was to "make government work better and cost less." The entrepreneurial government thus focused on outcomes, decentralized authority, reducing bureaucracy, and promoting competition.

New public management policies did offer citizens more influence through institutions like CDCs,[41] but NPM eventually came under fire, primarily for creating depoliticized spaces.[42] The National

Performance Review and similar initiatives placed citizens within the structures of the administration, but specific terms constrained their involvement. In this framework the government saw citizens as consumers and not as political subjects. Citizens were empowered to choose among different providers of public services and to give input on the provision of those services. But they had no role in deciding broader political questions. At the same time, governments privatized many public services through contracting out to private companies, and business assumed an expanding role in governance through public-private partnerships. The growing power of technical experts and professionals in government also worked to remove all technical matters from the administration's relationship with the consumer. Under the notion that the citizen had no information and in some cases lacked the ability to consider technical or procedural matters, many issues with direct consequences for the lives of the consumer were also removed to nonpublic places. Participatory processes during this time were largely disconnected from the political decisions of the administration, which only enhanced the power of the "professional" to the detriment of the citizen.[43]

An example of the limits of new public management is the way it dealt with citizen discontent about public schools in the United States. During the 1980s conservative "virtues of the market" became dominant in public discourse. Through school vouchers, for example, citizen discontent could be disaggregated into a matter of individual decision making—the schools parents sent their children to—and the problem could be resolved through a private decision rather than public, collective protest. In this way responsibility rested in the choices that citizens made rather than within public policy. This led to an erosion of a larger collective identity:

> The government's support of home mortgages, highway construction, and low gasoline taxes combined to create a nation of subur-

banites who pursued happiness and the good life not by pressing demands on local governments but by moving from one political jurisdiction to another. Instead of joining with neighbors to voice demands for better public services or amenities, they exercise the quiet, private "exit" option.[44]

These influences undermined any serious debate about what constitutes a good education or any broader policy issues.

Despite NPM's facilitation of civic engagement and attempts to steer the administration toward a consumption-oriented relationship with the individual, in the end it was not able to mitigate the problems of political disaffection. Not only that, but dissatisfaction with politics and political parties has been climbing steadily since that time.[45] As political disaffection continues, the problems originally associated with it persist: lack of political legitimacy, increased social demands, fragmentation, or populist tendencies of governments. NPM therefore did not resolve the problem; indeed it generated another: the privatization of the public realm.[46]

From New Public Management to Public Governance

By the early 2000s, however, scholars began to speak of and envision a new era of governance that was a direct reaction to NPM. This new form of governance, they predicted, would be one centered on citizenship, with its guiding principle the recuperation of debate and public life. Many scholars today speak of an era beyond NPM. As John Bryson, Barbara Crosby, and Laura Bloomberg observe, "Just as New Public Management supplanted traditional public administration in the 1980s and 1990s as the dominant view, a new movement is now under way that is likely to eclipse it."[47] Matt Leighninger, in his exemplary *Next Form of Democracy*, explains: "Twenty years ago, the Reaganite argued that 'big government is the problem'; ten years later, the Clintonites claimed that 'big government no longer exists.' Today, it is increasingly apparent that the size of government doesn't matter as much as how it connects with its constituents."[48]

New forms of governance seek to address the central problem of *connecting with constituents*. Since the mid-1990s scholars and others on both sides of the Atlantic had been sounding alarms over the state of citizen disaffection. Plummeting confidence in governance first caused concern in the 1990s when trust and faith in government affairs reached unprecedented lows. At that time scholars documented widespread disenchantment in the United States and around the world.[49] In the case of the United States, for example, political pulse takers of the time "registered record lows in political participation, record highs in public cynicism and alienation, and record rates of disapproval of the House of Representatives, the institution designed to present the public will."[50] In particular young Americans were found to be more cynical than the previous generation; they had a visceral dislike of politics, did not trust politicians, considered government unresponsive, believed average people did not have any political clout, and were skeptical because of the dominance of special interest groups. On both sides of the Atlantic citizens participated in a broad cultural conversation about the dangers of disaffection to the health of democracies.[51]

The book that best captured this sentiment was Robert Putnam's 2001 *Bowling Alone*. Putnam argued that under conditions of disaffection narrow and disgruntled forms of participation emerge, and these new forms are counter to public interest. Like Putnam many observers worried about unenthusiastic, privatist, or selfish kinds of citizen engagements that were emerging. In their view individuals in democracies were appearing to turn their back on the common good and beginning to think of the fulfillment of their political duties as a "troublesome annoyance."[52] In order for democracy to function properly, according to Putnam, modern democratic states require a counterbalancing set of political attitudes among their citizens.[53] Ultimately disaffection hinders productive social relations and erodes social capital in ways that are damaging to political life, perhaps even leading to regime failure.[54]

The early 2000s thus saw a series of concerted efforts on both sides of the Atlantic to transform political institutions and reconnect citizens to their governments. In Europe a number of countries abolished the council system, introduced direct elections of mayors, or adopted a hybrid system. Citizens also enacted policies to recall mayors and local politicians while establishing institutions of direct democracy.[55] The process of decentralization and the expansion of local political autonomy represented a nearly universal phenomenon across Europe. Scholars of European cities have shown how the EU has reshaped local governance crucially by strengthening the role of local governments and by creating a new set of common regulations and sources of funding.[56]

In the United States the expansion of citizen participation has been similar. Participatory efforts have been more fragmented but no less prevalent. Cities in large numbers began to experiment with different forms of collaborative or participatory governance beginning in the early 2000s.[57] There have also been a number of federal efforts, for example within the Environmental Protection Agency, which introduced two cross-program initiatives to make civic engagement and collaborative culture part of its mission. Its Innovation Action Council and National Advisory Council for Environmental Policy and Technology have opened a discussion about "reframing the agency's mission around stewardship and collaboration." These councils have catalyzed "local, state, and regional climate change partnerships" in ways the federal government can draw from to engage citizens in collaborative and participatory governance.[58]

This emerging model has been given a range of names and descriptors,[59] one of which is "public governance," a term that is a generalization of a still fragmented reality. The different versions of public governance share a set of principles: a recovery of the idea of the public sphere, collaboration, administrative holism, and an active citizenry. If new public management was a response to the inefficiencies of traditional public administration, public governance is a response to the "the narrowly utilitarian character of new public management."[60] Public governance usually links participatory democracy to the administration through the figure of the *stakeholder*, a model consistent with the philosophy that all groups should have a say in decisions that impact them.

A central tenet of this new governance is the possibility of win–win solutions that overcome the limits of traditionally conceived interest groups. Lisa Bingham, Tina Nabatchi, and Rosemary O'Leary catalog and describe the tools of this new governance, which include deliberative democracy, e-democracy, public conversations, participatory budgeting, citizen juries, study circles, collaborative policy making, and alternative dispute resolutions, all of which permit citizens and stakeholders to actively participate in the work of government. Even if these processes sometimes create conflict, new forms of governance resolve them: "By moving away from interest group competition toward consensus building, these new governance processes serve as mechanisms for cooperation and coordination among diverse and often rival participants in the policy process. As a result, these processes may increase the likelihood of a stable agreement."[61]

In the public governance model administrators themselves must adopt a different stance from their predecessors'. This requires a new leadership structure, centered not on older styles of personal leadership but on modes of articulation based on identities, norms, and institutions.[62] Leaders have to create participatory instances that are "open, welcoming, and informed, and where the contributions of each person are valued regardless of status or position."[63] Administrators should also practice (1) value-free neutrality, (2) legitimacy, "building authority and status for public administration in society," (3) sustainability, "finding a balance between economic development and the environment," (4) social equity, "seeking to deal with the impacts of the economic system on those at the lower end of the economic scale," and (5) the facilitation of citizen discourse, "to create an open and welcoming setting for self governance."[64]

The 2001 OECD report "Governance in the 21st Century," for example, explicitly signals this shift. The report is based on the "growing recognition that the ability or power of collective institutions to chart a particular course depends to an increasing degree on the active involvement of the governed."[65] Similarly the annual *World Development Report* from the World Bank has since the late 1990s also demonstrated increasing attention to the tenets of public governance, and clearly departs from ideas of minimal government while promoting the importance of giving the poor a voice through participatory governance. These documents and others value political participation and recognize that politics is about something more than the private citizen.

Public governance promotes citizen participation in the management of public affairs. It does not however totally reject the consumer-centered perspective. Yet unlike NPM, public governance rejects forms of public management derived exclusively from the logic of consumption. For public governance practitioners, democracy includes the political self-organization of citizens and self-government and thus implies political action toward public rather than private ends. Within the public governance model the citizen is a member of a political community that serves public and collective purposes, not only private consumption preferences. In sharp contrast to NPM the thinking behind public governance is that "governing is not the same as shopping or more broadly buying and selling goods."[66] A central concept of public governance is that politics is not just for political parties and interest groups and that citizens are *not* just customers. Public governance is grounded in an active citizenry that can play the valuable role of coordinating among different kinds of interests. Therefore within this model participation came to be seen as a valuable *complement* to government.

The advent of public governance is by no means a harbinger of NPM's disappearance. Recently, researchers analyzed the political programs of the Italian political parties through the prism of the two forms of governance. Their results showed the coexistence of both models across the programs, although the parties on the left had developed more intensive use of public governance-related ideas.[67]

This move toward public governance has not been without its critics either. One of the criticisms is that invocations of citizenry and participation do not guarantee democratic practice. The government of the United Kingdom for example is very active in the management of affairs guided by public governance and promoting participatory processes. The problem is that the initiatives are usually a top-down affair: the central government decides that municipalities should change their management approach. Meanwhile the central government has not modified the way it manages its resources, nor has it changed its concept of government—which remains much closer to NPM than to public governance—thus undermining any notion of social and political transformation.[68] In another example the center-left government of the Netherlands opened the parliamentary session in September 2013 by announcing the arrival of a new "participatory" era; but the content of their government program is marked by the cutback of welfare state provisions rather than the introduction of participatory governance. Just as with the participatory experiments carried out under NPM, these examples call into question whether putting the "citizen at the center" does not come at a cost of reducing the power and capacity of administrations.

Democratic Innovations Today

The waning of new public management's dominance and the advent of public governance in the late 1990s intensified the search for participatory instruments and widely expanded their use across the world.

In Europe and the United States cities have been the privileged locus for this kind of innovation. Though we cannot estimate the exact scope of their diffusion, according to the National League of Cities in the United States *80 percent* of municipalities in 2010 were carrying out participatory processes.[69] Similarly the vast majority of European cities today have implemented participatory mechanisms following legislative changes enacted to facilitate citizen involvement.[70] This was the case for example in the United Kingdom (Local Government Act, 2000), France (Proximity Democracy Law, 2002), Spain (Local Government Modernization Law, 2003), and the Netherlands (Local Democracy Law, 2002). Scholars have documented the proliferation of new participatory instruments in France, the United Kingdom, Spain, and many other countries.[71]

"Democratic innovations" covers a wide range of instruments: participatory budgets, citizen juries, deliberative surveys, referenda, town meetings, online citizen forums, e-democracy, public conversations, study circles, collaborative policy making, alternative dispute resolution, and so on. All of these represent a form of "participatory democracy" in the most literal sense of the term: citizens participating in government. These recent instruments aim to complement representative democracy rather than replace it, which was the goal of participatory democracy projects in social movements of the 1960s.[72] As we have discussed, this shift is propelled by the belief that democratic innovations can offer viable alternatives to the discontents of democracy,[73] an argument predicated on a specific reading of political developments over recent decades, according to which the problems of democracy can be resolved by more democracy. Such efforts, proponents believe, would lead to greater political awareness and engagement of the citizenry.[74]

The uniqueness of emerging democratic innovations is in part their ability to reach territories such as China and some countries in the Maghreb and the Middle East that from a democratic perspective have been historically unaffected by liberal traditions. Additionally their forms have been able to expand into economically fragile territories (Albania, Mozambique, the Dominican Republic) and cities both rich (Paris, New York, Edinburgh) and poor (Yaounde, Dakar). The International Observatory on Participatory Democracy's prize for the "best example of participatory practice" was awarded in 2014 to the municipality of Chengdu in China, which since 2009 has conducted a "Participatory Budgeting in Rural Services" project.[75] This project sets aside a portion of the rural services budget and entitles villagers the right to decide, monitor, and evaluate the project funds.[76]

But the key difference between democratic innovations and participatory democracy of the 1960s is the current emphasis on the active *incorporation* of the citizenry into the work of government rather than replacing that bureaucracy with an empowered community. This inclusion requires expanding the definition of the political subject to the whole civic body. Democratic innovations not only widen existing participatory channels; they also generate new structures intended for the entire citizenry.[77] This does not necessarily undermine existing social movements or civil society organizations that have some access to the state, but it does create a different political landscape in which *lay citizens* play a prominent role. In other words existing social movements may be included in the process but they no longer play a leading role. This shift and this new political subject do not represent a political break with current forms of democracy but rather an *improvement* of representative democracy.[78] As Brigitte Geissel notes, "These innovations can be regarded as supplements to representative democracy without turning representative democracy into a radically different 'strong' or 'participatory' democracy."[79] We borrow Geissel's useful classification of new participatory instruments, which she groups into three broad categories: *collaborative governance*, *deliberative procedures*, and *direct democracy*.[80]

Collaborative governance refers to initiatives that directly involve the citizenry in a public process of decision making. These are perhaps the most common and globalized kinds of initiatives because of their presumed ability to bring governments closer to citizens, disseminate new political skills among participants, build solidarity, and introduce a measure of transparency into government affairs. Some experiments following this model have significantly impacted the distribution of resources and the relations within civil society at the local level, but many others have had far less effect in both regards.[81] Scholars have noted that these initiatives have facilitated some change in existing political forms while also generating new conflicts.[82]

In only a few years participatory budgets (PB) have become one of the most notable instruments in processes of democratization. International agencies have broadly endorsed PB efforts and a growing number of experts and civil society organizations support them on the basis of their methods: inviting all citizens into new political spaces; including direct citizen participation in the management of public business; encouraging greater transparency; and promoting better distribution of public resources.

Deliberative procedures involve citizens in public debate on political matters but do not necessarily link them to decision-making processes. Deliberative procedures include citizen juries, deliberative circles, updated forms of town-hall meetings, and numerous online formats. While not quite as widespread or globalized as collaborative governance endeavors, they are a growing phenomenon. Unlike cases of collaborative governance deliberative procedures forefront deliberation itself. Sometimes these deliberations solve the problem of the relationship between representation and participation by using a draw to select random samples of the population. This selective sampling provides a way around the key problem of participatory governance: the legitimacy of the participating voices.[83] In most cases participants are selected by lot, receive technical and specialized information about a problem, and are then invited to deliberate together on the issue before making a final decision.

The government in British Columbia, Canada, used deliberative procedures to propose a reform to the electoral process.[84] Local governments around the world have also used this mechanism to deal with important issues at the municipal level. Deliberative instruments offer the possibility of rigorous and serious deliberation. They bring together technical and citizen expertise to enable citizens to actively participate in theoretically sophisticated processes. These instruments' weaknesses arise from the difficulty of linking the experiments to the public decision-making process. And deliberative procedures generate a recurring set of questions: can everybody speak; is the process manipulated; are the participants truly representative of the population as a whole, and so forth.[85]

Finally the instruments of *direct democracy*, such as referenda, invite the citizens to decide directly on a specified political issue. Direct democracy covers those instruments that involve the citizenry in public debate on political matters, but it is not necessarily linked to a structured decision-making process as with citizen juries. Critics of direct democracy's instruments argue that this process does not allow for intensive deliberation. Participants, critics point out, do not engage in debate but remain passive receivers of third-party messages. Individuals make decisions based on personal considerations, and the results of all participants are then aggregated. Nevertheless some research supports the benefit of direct democracy's resulting political situation, in which citizens learn to pay closer attention to the public realm and thus keep a closer watch on government. This awareness raises the standard of analysis and increases political debate among citizens. Switzerland, with its long tradition of referenda, has further institutionalized the referendum as a form of government in recent years, and the majority of OECD member countries have incorporated institutional changes intended to facilitate the use of referenda. In Germany citizens began to participate in legislative initiatives ten years ago to exercise more political control over mayors. The local government has simplified the procedures required to introduce legislative changes and there has been an increase in the number of local referenda in recent years.

Participation's Ambiguities

These democratic innovations transform the questions we are able to ask about democracy, principally because of the political subject they presuppose (the citizenry), the style of politics they imply (around points of agreement rather than points of conflict), and the specific instruments they bring into play, the majority of them aimed at resolving problems within a deliberative framework. It is worth returning for a moment to the question of political coordination, our concern in this book with how identities and interests are coordinated in a democracy. Contemporary participation is founded on three ambiguous coordinating principles: *deliberation; the importance of unmediated voice;* and *the inclusion of all voices.*

The first principle is deliberation. All of these participatory instruments promote, in one way or another, collective participation as a means to reach agreements. Policy derives from the citizenry rather than from sectoral interests and seeks to avoid conflict in the construction of the common will. Whereas once the idea of the market enabled NPM to deal with the problem of articulating disparate individual interests in a fluid society, now discussion enables such coordination. Instead of worrying about addressing individual preferences, the central preoccupation today is around defining a regulated space within which citizens can debate the public good in a communicative manner.

If new public management drew from rational choice theory, public governance today draws from deliberative theory. NPM treated participants as consumers of government services who were rational and profit maximizing, and thus promoted narrow forms of participation by individuals with specific objectives. Public governance has instead relied on an alternative framework that imagines individuals as reflective agents with unfixed preferences who are prepared to debate and change their views during the process of deliberation. The ideal participant is an individual who learns, changes her opinion, and makes decisions accordingly.[86]

But this is ambiguous. On one hand, equality becomes a central issue. Participatory institutions create horizontal spaces in which participants can express themselves on the same political platform. This calls into question the privileged position of technical expertise and places value on common sense and the ordinary knowledge of citizens. It thus transforms the role of technical expertise into one serving the process of discussion rather than acting as a source of final decisions. In addition the basic idea that individuals might become active agents in the practical formulation of laws and regulations sharply contrasts with liberal traditions that assume the division of political labor between representatives and the represented as the central dynamic of the political system.[87]

On the other hand, if the idea of deliberative democracy and the communicative individual can raise questions about equality, technical expertise, and representative democracy itself, it also has the potential to stifle communication. Precisely because deliberative democracy relies on a reflective individual who can change her preferences, critics argue it can become a means of *depoliticizing* certain questions. Deliberative democracy focuses on norms of civility and discourse, on appropriate modes of conduct, and it privileges the changeability of preferences. Thus some see it as especially compatible with the reproduction of social hierarchies. One particularly poignant criticism asserts that deliberative democracy may at best create the fiction of rational deliberation that in fact justifies an elitist and male-centered kind of citizenship. A more sinister evaluation of deliberative democracy's weaknesses is that its public justification aspect could be used to lend legitimacy to certain inequalities. In other words deliberative democracy processes might attempt to solve a particular problem without confronting the need to influence larger systems of administrative organization.[88]

A second principle of coordination is that of direct, unmediated communication. It is not uncommon for promoters of participation today to frame their appeals in terms of going beyond unions, traditional neighborhood associations, or interest groups. New democratic institutions thus rely on unmediated forms of participation, placing much emphasis on "regular citizens." Against the "civil society argument" in which social organizations themselves structure public opinion, it is the unorganized citizenry who directly contribute to structure the political system through specific participatory institutions. There is no negotiation with mediating organizations. Instead citizens participate in collective decision making, which directly assimilates into the political system. Thus democratic innovations change the political subject and widen the political boundaries to include lay citizens. These innovations do not just transform social organizations; they also change the structures of collective negotiation between the organizations and the public authorities with a direct system of decision making.

This emphasis on the lay citizen is partially meant to respond to criticisms in the 1990s about professional activism,[89] and the worry that volunteerism had become an activity for the middle classes and the rich or for those with more educational resources and better political skills.[90] To some extent new participatory institutions also draw inspiration from what social scientists sometimes call "non-conventional forms of participation,"[91] or forms of participation outside of institutions or formal organizations. These include petitions, consumer boycotts, and direct action protests.[92]

But direct participation is at its core also ambiguous. On one hand, to emphasize direct voice undoubtedly structures political relations in a way that emphasizes potentially democratizing horizontal relationships. It implies a political agenda of a kind of decentered political action that directly involves the citizenry, relegating the experts to the role of providing information. On the other hand, the emphasis on direct voice could conflict with existing associations that address similar issues. Associational life is normatively prized not for its ability to represent all but for its ability to amplify certain underprivileged voices. Iris Young, for example, criticizes deliberative procedures that are open to all citizens, because for her these procedures further marginalize those already underrepresented in the public sphere.[93]

A third principle of coordination is voice for all, itself an incorporation of radical democratic principles of participation. This principle results from a gradual evolution of political thought that has been taking place since the 1960s.[94] The protests and collective forums that emerged in the 1960s against the political and economic elites shared a participatory vision. The graffiti in Paris in 1968 and the Students for a Democratic Society's "Port Huron Statement" in the United States cried out for participatory democracy; they imagined a utopia that took as its point of reference a society in which everyone had an equal voice.[95] The 1960s brought to the surface a critique devoted to the democratization of all spheres of politics and positioned itself against any kind of political elitism or oligarchic organization. As the "Port Huron Statement" put it, the goal was to share in the decision making that impacted their lives, and that "decision-making of basic social consequence be carried on by public groupings."[96]

As the protests of the 1960s faded, this perspective all but disappeared from view, taking refuge in social movements on the periphery of the political system.[97] These groups, operating from an ideological position rooted in autonomy, solidarity, and democracy, maintained a discourse against neoliberalism, capital, and the elite dominance of institutions. However, they established themselves across the global map, generally moving away from local struggles.[98] During the 1990s this broad movement expanded and began to impact international debate with its critique of the injustices arising from the links between governance and global institutions.[99] These groups were able to create an international political network that came together to protest international meetings of economic organizations like the IMF and the G8. The tactics of these alter-globalization movements owed much to the democratizing spirit of the 1960s, as did the central claim: international institutions were broken because they served elite interests and denied the voice of the disenfranchised over decisions of common interest.

But if the idea of inclusion of alter-globalization movements, or of Paris '68 for that matter, implied a powerful sense of collective fate and *collective control of institutions*, under the "new spirit of government" inclusion has become reduced to a shared collective fate only. It is an important principle for participatory instruments to be broadly inclusive, and it is against this standard that they are often measured; but the hearing out of all voices does not imply that these voices have power over decisions that affect them.

These principles of coordination highlight both the potential and the limits of this age of participation. The principles serve as frameworks of justification that determine the possibilities of legitimacy of the participatory devices launched.[100] Thus they generate critical standards against which instruments are tested. Are participatory processes truly deliberative? Do they provide the possibility of truly unmediated participation? Are they really inclusive? These are nontrivial questions which show the distance that separates participatory processes and their potential, thereby requiring promoters to justify their initiatives from these principles. Governments are forced to incorporate a horizontal space where citizens have a direct voice and spaces oriented to the common good. Moreover these principles can always be put to use by participants demanding a deepening of participatory mechanisms.

Empowerment within Limits

Mayor de Blasio's administration is emblematic of participation's wide appeal today and of the three principles of coordination we have discussed as central: deliberation, direct participation, and voice for all. Many of the administrative efforts under this leadership incorporate direct, deliberative participation with the purpose of giving a voice to all New Yorkers. Mayor de Blasio symbolically supports policies that put ordinary citizens at the center of his administration.

Talking Transition set the tone for the administration and it was described as "possibly the largest, best-connected attempt to use a poll to shape New York government policy."[101] Mayor de Blasio has also endorsed and promoted participatory budgeting as a grassroots effort to shape policy without political corruption and opaque games, and he describes such efforts as "a wave of the future."[102] One of the first initiatives that de Blasio launched, in partnership with the municipal administrations of Chicago and Los Angeles, was the "Cities for Citizenship" (C4C) program. The program seeks to strengthen the links between marginalized communities, the city, and its services.[103] All told, de Blasio's new politics of inclusion seeks to curtail both the technocratic vision and elite privilege of previous administrations, preferring instead to connect his administration directly with the public. The connection to citizens and the search for new tools to facilitate their direct influence on public policies signal a shift in the administration and indicate a vision of a city for all, not only the most privileged.

Yet this call for the involvement of citizens is fundamentally ambivalent. These modes of inclusion negate conflict and present the debate between different political policies as a neutral choice between competing ideas. More than focusing on enemies (say the "1%" as in his campaign slogans), Mayor de Blasio imagines allies and seeks to build an imaginary city where citizens share interests. This vision could signify the gradual emptying of the political sphere in favor of technical discussions on the best possible decisions, foreclosing political conflict, avoiding new visions, and ultimately eliminating dissidence. This new way of doing politics could also become the next banality of politics.

Talking Transition, for example, was intended "to provide data" to improve the performance of elected representatives in the new administration, while participatory budgeting is considered the ideal instrument to "take the public money wherever it is needed." "Cities for Citizenship" programs include new ways of including the needs of marginalized New Yorkers in planning exercises. While these projects are indeed a more transparent way to collect and apply data, the new mantra of doing policy "without political influence, without playing the game, without corruption" seduces us with the vision of a postpolitical utopia where profane versions of politics—interests, conflict, division, disagreement—have no place. Governance in this vein threatens to become, in the words of Rancière, "the art of suppressing the political. It is a procedure of self-subtraction."[104]

Projects like Talking Transition can succeed in building bridges with citizens in an era marked by political disaffection. But if we focus only on people's needs and the new tools designed to attend to them, the process of political empowerment becomes vague. Critics of "postpolitics," like Rancière, worry that contemporary polities have displaced procedures for conflicts in the name of democracy and civility. The seeming neutrality of participatory instruments can camouflage a political process that exploits spaces populated by theoretical equals while exerting power in line with dominant knowledge.[105]

The paradigm shift toward public governance we have described has made it easier to envision and implement citizen-centric institutions based on inclusion and direct access. We have no doubt that these processes will survive only if they embrace the idea of continually broadening democratic boundaries. Yet participants in the processes cannot actually go beyond the boundaries of the process itself. They usually cannot make significant decisions, let alone change the terms of participation or the administration. Even when administrations are willing to open up participatory spaces, these spaces often remain marginal, prompting many to question whether we can associate social or political transformation with this new way of doing politics. From this perspective it is clear that the ideology of inclusion can be met without demanding major structural changes.

De Blasio and his administration face a dilemma emanating from the limits of the empowerment processes generated by their very own participatory programs. As long as we speak of processes conceived and driven by administrators, a number of serious questions remain. Are these processes in fact capable of transforming politics? Do citizens truly have a voice in political and public affairs? Does these processes have any influence on the public good? The remainder of the book is designed to explore these questions and the ambivalences that emerge around empowerment processes that take place within the limits set by administrators. The fundamental contradiction of democratic innovations like talking governance is that they invite participation to debate the common good but do not endow ordinary citizens with the power to determine outcomes. This is empowerment, but within limits.

Nevertheless, we also believe that attempts to create a political landscape based on agreements between equals can facilitate the emergence of new relations that do empower citizens. The remaining chapters approach this problem through the case of participatory budgeting, one of the most globalized examples of a participatory template.

The unfolding of this first experiment reveals clear controversies that occurred both within the Porto Alegre administration and outside of it. Subsequent implementations of participatory budgeting tempered many of these internal and external tensions as it traveled to the Global North. By looking closely at the conflicts generated by these fairly circumscribed participatory projects, we seek to make a broader point about the role of such democratic innovations in contemporary societies, about their potentials as well as their clear limits.

CHAPTER THREE

The Global Spread of Participation

When you ask people about Participatory Budgeting, it's a little bit like the Rorschach Ink-Blot Test. You're learning something about the people that you're talking to.

—*Brian Levy, World Bank Institute, Governance Unit*[1]

The World Bank occupies an imposing building of glass and steel on a corner of Pennsylvania Avenue not far from the White House. In May 2007 the World Bank Institute convened a meeting to develop recommendations for a participatory budgeting campaign in Africa. Participatory budgeting (PB), as we have mentioned, is a template for citizen input into public budgets that had been developed in Brazil in the late 1980s and had since the early 2000s attracted a great deal of international attention. For two days Brazilian consultants and representatives from Latin American and African NGOs, together with the bank's own civic empowerment team, discussed the benefits of PB, Brazilian best practices, and feasibility issues for an African context. Later in the year the Bank sponsored a PB workshop in Johannesburg followed by a distance-learning program to disseminate PB throughout much of the continent. Hundreds of participants throughout Africa took part in one of the trainings or conferences.

Less than a mile away from the World Bank on the other side of the Potomac River are the modest offices of Tenants and Workers United

(TWU), a small and mostly volunteer-run organization. Founded in 1990 to "to build the power of low-income people" and to "struggle against racism and sexism," TWU provides legal assistance to immigrants, language classes, and education on tenants' rights.[2] It is perhaps best known for its work in the late 1990s, launching one of the first successful "living wage" campaigns in the United States.[3] TWU also organizes direct action campaigns on social justice issues. In late 2006 some staff members, after attending the World Social Forum in Brazil, became interested in participatory budgeting. They developed research materials and started conversations about the feasibility of a PB campaign for the DC area. In 2007 TWU was one of the founding organizations of a national social justice network, the Right to the City (RTTC). RTTC was founded to "strategically challenge neoliberal economic policies."[4] Most RTTC members agreed on the value of participatory budgeting, and the U.S. Social Forum prominently featured PB that year.

The World Bank and TWU are vastly dissimilar institutions pursuing fundamentally different projects, working at different scales, and connecting with very different publics. Looking more closely at how the two organizations discuss PB reveals an unsurprising difference in their visions of participation. World Bank documents emphasize how PB can be put to work for better governance, while TWU imagines it will be part of a redistribution of power in society. But what is surprising are the striking *similarities* in how these two organizations describe participatory budgeting itself: a sequence of open meetings to discuss projects and needs, followed by an open and transparent system for vote taking, eventually leading to a budget that reflects the voters' preferences. What is it about participatory budgeting that attracts both leftist social justice organizations like TWU and transnational development agencies like the World Bank? How is it that this kind of participation became so malleable, so polyvalent, that it could

be understood to be part of such different (and some would say opposing) projects?

Clearly something about PB resonates with the current moment
of retrenched national states and broad dissatisfaction with governments. Today common sense around governance emphasizes that "big
government" is not able to cope with modern problems. This line of
thinking implicates "bloated bureaucracies" and "red tape" in governments' inefficiencies and inadequacies. But as the capacities of governments in the Global North have diminished, the *meaning* of government has changed as well.[5] This redefinition is linked to a rationality of
government that emphasizes decentralization, horizontal linkages, and
societal creativity.[6] The ethos of the new spirit of government, which
revolves around a citizen-centered and "networked pattern of coordination of collective action," has replaced traditional government and
given the "ordinary citizen" a privileged new place in administration.[7]
The rapid diffusion of democratic innovations throughout the world
speaks to the nature of our rapidly expanding communications and
increasingly intermeshed networks in the globalized era.[8] But more
than that, looking at the story of PB points to how ideas—specifically
ideas about governing and running social affairs—travel today.

The Thing That Worked

The story of participatory budgeting begins in Porto Alegre in the
south of Brazil, where the first participatory budgeting assemblies were
held in late 1989. But the roots of the story can be located a few years
earlier, in 1985. At the time Brazil was transitioning from a military
dictatorship to a democracy, and the first free mayoral elections since
the military coup of 1964 were scheduled for November. In October,
in anticipation of the first free election, Porto Alegre community activists met with the Porto Alegre mayoral candidates. These activists
had no idea how the content of their discussion that evening would

eventually resonate around the world over the next quarter century. The activists had gathered to pose a slate of questions about social movements to each of the candidates. For example, they asked: "How would the candidate, as mayor, improve public housing or transportation?" Following an idea previously endorsed by neighborhood associations, they also asked if the candidates would implement community control over municipal finances.[9] However, the candidate elected mayor, who came from the Labor Party (PDT) and had gestured support toward participation, did not create the desired institutions. It was the mayor elected in the following election, from the Workers' Party (*Partido dos Trabalhadores*, or PT), who ultimately set in motion a process of community control. By 1991 the mayor's administration had implemented something called "participatory budgeting," and by 1992 observers were noting its success: meetings were well attended and participants decided on projects that were then passed on to the city managers. By 1993 it was an unequivocal success with massive participation and dozens of projects underway. Porto Alegre's administrators managed to achieve something that had eluded leftists up to that point: the combination of good governance, redistribution, and political good fortunes. This success led to the party's reelection.

The story so far is generally well known: urban social movements introduced an idea, the Workers' Party government took it up, it *worked,* and then it went on to travel the world.[10] Most accounts of this project generally miss two important elements, which we emphasize here. First, when the Porto Alegre administration translated the original idea from urban social movements and filtered it through administrative policy, one fundamental element changed: the experiment deemphasized the role of existing associations and their leaders in favor of the individual citizen. Second, participatory budgeting was not the experiment's only success: it was an integral part of an entirely novel yet effective administrative project. Although from the point of view of participants PB was perhaps the most visible part, it was not the only or most important part. Yet international researchers and networks took up this particular element.

The Individual–Association Pendulum

The Right to the City's 2007 proposal for participatory budgeting included a few central rules common to similar projects: meetings must be open to everyone and people must participate as individuals, not as representatives of say a neighborhood association or a union. By now these seem like self-evident features of the process and of democratic innovations in general. But the urban social movements of Brazil in the late 1980s and the Workers' Party that implemented PB in Porto Alegre would not have expected these conditions.

Social movements and other urban organizations' original proposals for participatory budgeting processes imagined that citizen participation be based on *associational representation*. That is, these groups envisioned representatives from existing organizations debating budget priorities. A document from the time, presented to mayoral candidates in 1986 by the city's neighborhood associations (UAMPA), exemplifies this well. The document called for a system "where the investment priorities of each district would be discussed with popular leaders of each district."[11] Each district, according to this document, would include a "Popular Council with proportional representation of the community movement."[12] In this vision representatives of clubs, churches, and associations would come together in a forum to debate proposals.[13] One of the key principles of Porto Alegre's 1990 participatory budgeting process, in contrast, was individual participation, that is, "meetings open to anyone" and any citizen—associated or not— could come to the meeting and have an equal voice. The distance between the two visions, between the initial civil society proposal and the ultimate execution, was immense and profoundly consequential.[14]

How did this change happen? Early on, organized urban social movements and the newly elected administration came in conflict over several issues, the first of which was municipal bus services. Ten days into the Workers' Party mandate, administrators found themselves in a controversy with neighborhood associations and unions over bus fares and the wages of bus drivers and conductors. The administration had taken over bus services and created a municipal bus company as promised in campaign materials. However, it soon clashed with the community movement (who wanted lower fares) and the unions (who wanted higher wages for drivers and conductors). The administrators, on the other hand, felt their priority was to maintain uninterrupted service. The administration held to its position and swiftly dismissed striking employees who were sabotaging bus routes. This caused a furor from the national federation of labor, which quickly released a series of condemning statements.

The relationship between the Workers' Party administration and organized community movements continued to sour after the municipal bus incidents, and the organized community movement started to openly criticize the administration over perceived shortcomings.[15] Vice Mayor Tarso Genro defended the administration's position on the bus strikes, arguing that public administrators "have to respond to the demands, thinking of the whole of society, and not only one segment."[16] These and other public statements signaled an important shift in thinking on the part of leftist administrators. Collectives like unions, which were previously understood as privileged interlocutors, became symbolically reduced to a segment smaller than the whole, rather than a representative of the whole.[17]

These tensions between organized movements and the administration manifested again when the administration organized a seminar to decide the basic outline of the new participatory process in June 1989. Some activists from community movements felt betrayed by the administration. At the same time city hall was becoming increasingly ambivalent toward "organized civil society."[18] A charged debate occurred between those who thought that movements should have a privileged place in the new process and those who favored individual participation. One discarded proposal, for example, outlined a process that would be run entirely through neighborhood associations, with assigned seats for presidents of existing neighborhood associations.

The process that eventually emerged in late 1989 was based on a compromise. The agreement determined that meetings were open to all, but the Union of Neighborhood Associations would play a prominent role. The city was divided into five districts and a meeting was held in each. Representatives of the Union of Neighborhood Associations facilitated and organized some of these. At each meeting facilitators collected demands for projects from attendees and these were voted on; each district elected three representatives to form a council to carry on discussions. Even though nearly one thousand participants attended these assemblies, internal evaluations from the time considered this modified PB process a failure. In one district no one participated. In at least one other district, where civil society was well organized, the meeting became hostile when activists demanded that city hall turn over the running of all government functions to local social movements. The activists ended the meeting by walking out. For some in the Porto Alegre administration the walkout and the hostility fostered more suspicion about the political motives of the heads of neighborhood associations.[19] For others it was proof that social movements would not be able to self-mobilize organically, and when they did, their demands might be more immediate and more confrontational than administrators might like.

From 1990 onward things were different. The Porto Alegre administration continued to strengthen its stance on individual participation. It divided the city into sixteen districts with the intent to reach areas with unorganized residents. The administration rewrote the rules of the participatory process to clearly specify that associations would play no formal role. It instituted a new Council of the Budget to oversee the whole process, with two representatives per district and, as a concession, one representative from the Union of Neighborhood Associations and one from the Municipal Employees' Union. These two seats were eventually discarded as well.[20]

This new process was thus something of a novelty. The procedures intended to solicit the participation of ordinary citizens and allow them to debate the general interest as a new form of management of public affairs. It did not go against associations per se, but it challenged their monopoly over representing the people or the idea that they represented all citizens. But it also required new administrative habits to handle this new political subject (all citizens). This change was a significant turn away from an administrative apparatus developed around privileged interlocutors.

Administrative Reform and a New Public Sphere

In his recollections of the process of developing participatory budgeting, former vice mayor (and later mayor) Raul Pont described a sense of newness and invention with everything that the administration did.[21] Brazil, Pont noted, did not have traditions of direct democracy to draw on, so everything had to be new.[22] PB was understood not only as an invitation for people to participate but as part of a comprehensive set of reforms designed to introduce a wholly new way of governing.

Yet within this new context of PB the Porto Alegre administration closed nearly all other channels for citizen demand making. The population could only contact the administration through the process of PB initiatives.[23] Everyone could participate (both the poor and the wealthy, the associated and the nonassociated), and there were no other privileged channels for the wealthy or the politically aligned. In this way it circumvented politicians and cronyism, but it also cut out urban social movements and protest tactics as a way to make demands. A leader of the community movement at the time recalled that urban social movements felt marginalized because "when any [of] our demands reached the city councilors," their response was that we had to "go to the PB to get anything done about it."

In order for "participation to come into the administration" new patterns and practices were created *within* the administration. The administration achieved this through a combination of "political centralization with administrative decentralization."[24] The mayor created a budget planning office that centralized management accounts and PB; administratively it was positioned *above* municipal departments. The idea was to "ring-fence" the capital budget from other sources of pressure. By privileging the office above municipal departments, the administration ensured impartiality in implementation. Brazilian administrations are notoriously fragmented, with groups within political parties (or parties themselves) occupying and exerting control over particular departments.[25] Traditionally in Brazil, becoming a department head in a prominent municipal department (like one in charge of public housing or infrastructure) was often seen as a stepping-stone in one's political career toward becoming a member of city council or mayor. Control from above helped prevent policy implementation from becoming currency in the jockeying for political power. And the establishment of a centralized planning department above municipal departments introduced an element of coordination between local districts.

Thus in Porto Alegre centralization of planning was combined with a decentralization of the administrative machinery. The administration required all municipal departments to create positions for community facilitators. Community facilitators were the "face" of each municipal department in each of the city's districts. They attended all PB meetings with the express purpose of helping participants prepare technically viable projects and to be accountable for ongoing projects. That is, they were responsible for interfacing between community and technical experts within the departments. All community facilitators attended a weekly forum to synthesize participatory processes. About this effort, one facilitator reflected, "technical expertise was to be made subservient to the popular mandate, and not the other way around."

The mayor's administration also introduced significant tributary and fiscal reform to increase revenues. It was a "rigorous policy of cutting current expenditures" combined with tax reforms and measures to improve tax administration.[26] This included introducing progressivity in the two most important municipal taxes: real estate and services. It also meant updating utilities and increasing control over tax fraud.[27] The city's financial capacity increased as a result, essentially doubling the city's income over the next ten years. Porto Alegre's own revenues accounted for almost 60 percent of its budget by the late 1990s, freeing up millions for new investments that PB committees would decide upon. This level of local fiscal reform almost mirrored that of some European cities.[28]

These administrative reforms made participatory budgeting possible and successful. As is well known, thousands of participants eventually took part in PB meetings: a multitude of Porto Alegre's poorer citizens participated in a relatively simple system that promised and delivered results. Many poor urban denizens who otherwise had little voice in government or political affairs became apt and loyal participants. Week after week they diligently attended meetings and debated the arcana of municipal finances and regulations. These otherwise marginal citizens decided on investment priorities for their neighborhoods, boroughs, and the city itself. The reforms enhanced the administrative machinery, improved the conditions of the poor, and established a new way of administering that would eventually inspire admiration elsewhere.

But the process was not without its detractors. For neighborhood leaders accustomed to the "dance" of protest and favor trading (and privileged access to clientelist politicians), the process closed privileged channels of communication. More radical activists found the process too limited. For some the experience imbued participation with a different logic. PB focused on resolving the specific issues of life in the city rather than, in the words of an activist at the time, "attacking the core problems: how the city was financed [and] what model of the state we want." Another activist leader recalled that it was "a space of joint management with the government in which certain demands could *not* be made." It appeared to be a contradiction to debate a "scant municipal resource, fighting for a piece of the budget, instead of debating the financing of the city itself."[29]

These sentiments highlight some of the unintended consequences of PB as a form of democratization from above. PB was intended to give civil society a new role in public affairs, and it replaced informal debates with formal deliberation. Instead of the occasionally chaotic world of social movement discussion, PB introduced rule-bound meetings. But this was premised on accepting certain limits of public debate based on administrative limits, schedules, and priorities. Many questions—for example what kind of alternative state models activists could imagine—fell by the wayside.

Another dilemma had to do with the recognition of collective actors, or the question of who was entitled to speak on behalf of a neighborhood.[30] In the PB framework there was a disconnect between official and legitimate representation of the citizenry. That is, the permitted, official representation of the citizenry in the PB process (all citizens on equal footing) did not correspond to representation that had organically emerged from within neighborhoods over the years (certain individuals as selected representatives). For many neighborhood leaders PB represented an administrative attempt to break the back of associations and their autonomy by disrespecting their own criteria for participation and representation. One neighborhood leader recalled that "it had taken me a lot to become president of the association . . . and they wanted me to go and discuss things with other people who had done nothing to get there."[31]

Despite these criticisms PB was a success, especially as it proved politically efficacious: the Workers' Party administration was comfortably reelected in 1992, 1996, and 2000. Each time, the party advertised PB as the centerpiece of a mode of governance that benefited the whole city. The Porto Alegre PB framework was entirely new, but it quickly met a national and then an international audience. Practitioners soon turned it into a traveling blueprint. As it traveled, the idea of participatory democracy became a new and pragmatic blueprint of governance.

Becoming a Best Practice

Participatory budgeting as a model of participatory democracy spread quickly. We identify at least two phases of its broadening circulation. First, it diffused throughout Brazil, and to a lesser extent Latin America, up through the mid-1990s. During this period the idea traveled through networks associated with the Workers' Party and allied NGOs as a success story of "how the left can govern." The "Porto Alegre story" became emblematic in the 1990s of how the party—and by extension the left—could not only govern but govern well. Then in the late 1990s PB began to travel the globe in a more reduced form.

For it to become a model within Brazil, PB had to first be distilled into a set of principles that could work in different places. This transformation took place through national conversations about participation under leftist administrations. In 1990 Workers' Party administrators along with academics and movement and NGO activists formed a national network to exchange experiences and debate the merits of different participatory experiments. The National Forum on

Popular Participation in Democratic and Popular Administrations, the FNPP, started to convene on a regular basis. Early on, the FNPP was the site of a heated controversy between advocates of different forms of participation, some favoring preexisting community movements more than others. One administrator recalled that in administrative exchanges with other cities, Porto Alegre's process always displayed two particular dimensions: the comprehensive administrative reforms and the administration's rejection of associational representation.[32] At this time some other cities had already begun to model their processes on Porto Alegre's. And between 1993 and 1996 several other Workers' Party administrations experimented with participatory formats. By 1996 it seemed clear that those with Porto Alegre-style PB seemed to fare much better than those following other models. The Porto Alegre administration's success in continuing to draw participants and win reelection again in 1995 stood in sharp contrast to several other Workers' Party administrations in Brazil that failed to win reelection, sometimes spectacularly. By 1996 the FNPP settled on PB as its principal prescription while scholars and practitioners identified the "Porto Alegre model" as the primary inspiration for PB.

The model traveled and worked in different contexts within Brazil. The FNPP and other national NGOs, like IBASE and Fundação Getúlio Vargas, started to track and disseminate PB practices. Due in no small part to the work of the FNPP and groups like it, 103 administrations introduced PB between 1997 and 2000, and at least 150 more did so in 2001–4. Almost all of these drew direct inspiration if not downright technical assistance from Porto Alegre. The PB that traveled, however, did so as part of a bundle of administrative reforms and as part of a political project. Most of the cities that implemented it at the time also implemented several of the administrative reforms described above.

Increasingly within Brazil participatory budgeting became linked with good governance and was promoted as having a beneficial impact on city government. An FNPP how-to guide asserts that participatory budgeting can serve as "an efficient instrument" to achieve goals like "greater transparency in the budget," "more social control of public finances," "meeting the needs of the poorer populations," "fighting clientelism and corruption," "increasing the legitimacy of municipal administrations," "sharing of power," "the strengthening of cooperation," "education for citizenship," and "the broadening of the public sphere."[33] The document signals an important shift: if in Porto Alegre participatory budgeting broke with the imaginary that associated participation with populism and economic inefficiency, now it was also becoming something else. The benefits of participatory budgeting in this version rely on a mix of good governance (such as transparency), social justice, and civic goals (such as cooperation).

Around this time, significantly, PB began to lose its exclusive identification with the Workers' Party. According to Brian Wampler and Leonardo Avrtizer, for example, by 2001 center and right parties were responsible for over 40 percent of PB experiments.[34] Prize committees started to link these participatory experiments with "cities that work," calling them "islands of efficiency."[35] These included significant citizen participation on issues besides budgeting, such as environmental action, health provisions, and use of computer resources at the municipal level.[36]

Going Global and the Dissemination of the Instrument

The late 1990s and early 2000s were very busy and internationally prominent for Porto Alegre city officials as participatory budgeting started to travel globally. In 1998 *Le Monde Diplomatique* had run the first of a series of articles extolling participatory budgeting, while a book by the former mayor of Porto Alegre, Tarso Genro, and Ubiratan de Souza, describing participatory budgeting, was translated and republished in several countries in Europe the next year.[37] These came on the heels of the 1996 UN-Habitat Conference, where Porto Alegre's participatory budgeting won recognition as one of the "42 best practices of urban governance."[38] Together the *Le Monde* pieces, the book, and the United Nations prize were widely credited for putting participatory budgeting on the global map of innovations. In those years Porto Alegre incumbents started to be invited across the Atlantic to discuss their successes, becoming "ambassadors of participation," in Oliveira's phrase.[39]

In those years, too, in Porto Alegre participatory budgeting became the Workers' Party administration's "calling card," and administrators played no small role in its internationalization. This promotion was varied, including actively competing in international good governance competitions. As Vanessa Marx has documented, the city's Office of International Cooperation emerged as an adjunct to its Community Relations Office, the frontline office that dealt with participatory budgeting.[40] Two defining events took place in the city thanks to party involvement in international networks. They describe well the ambivalences of PB—its intention to combine in one instrument the political imaginary of participatory democracy and social movements from the left, and the efficiency justification of administration. At the end of the 1990s these were key moments for the globalization of PB.

In 1999 the city hosted the first International Seminar on Participatory Democracy, which had in attendance representatives of the United Nations Development Programme (UNDP), the Inter-American Development Bank, and the World Bank. That the list of attendees included these organizations surprised some observers at the time.

Yet the presence of World Bank representatives at an event on participatory democracy marked the culmination of the change in thinking of global agencies, which had been afoot for some years. In the late 1990s multilateral agencies were particularly interested in solutions to development problems. Of course to some extent the UNDP and World Bank have been interested in participation since the 1970s.[41] But the late 1990s was a distinct period; development thinking was

experiencing a tectonic shift. Among development experts was a growing recognition that the structural adjustment programs of the 1980s
had collapsed and that "state-dominated development has failed, but so
will stateless development."[42] Development agencies' thinking shifted at
this time decisively toward an emphasis on good, local governance. The
World Bank's *World Development Report* clearly emphasized this shift.
One report in 1999/2000 devoted an entire chapter to decentralization,
valuing local solutions and well-functioning institutions more positively
than before.[43] This movement toward participation has been similar in
the Global North. Economic and international agencies started to shift
the standards of government to include participation as a solution to the
increasing problems of legitimacy of governance in developed countries.
As the OECD report *Citizens as Partners* argued, the increasing complexity of solutions, the challenges in answering to citizens' demands,
and the need to implement strategic and long-term policies demanded
more citizen involvement in government.[44] Participatory methods came
to be valued as a complement to good local governance. These methods
led to "greater efficiency and effectiveness of investment and contribut-
ing to processes of democratization and empowerment,"[45] while promoting transparent, accountable, and participatory institutions.[46] PB
experiments adopted the language of participation and empowerment.

While participatory budgeting was only one participatory method
of interest to international agencies, they devoted significant resources
to understand, promote, and diffuse it throughout the developing
world. International agencies' efforts in this direction included the
Urban Management Program of the United Nations in Latin America and in the Caribbean (PGU-ALC) and the URB-AL European
program, which highlighted PB as a best practice. This U.N.-backed
network sponsored dozens of international events while producing
"practical tools and materials" and offering training programs. At its
height the URB-AL Network-9 had a budget of five million euros and

involved 450 local governments on both sides of the Atlantic. In 2008 it went so far as to offer an international online master's degree in participatory budgeting, based on stays in Porto Alegre and then other participating partner cities such as Córdoba and Florence in Europe or Rosario and Cuenca in Latin America.[47]

In 2001 the World Social Forum was held in Porto Alegre for the first time. Alter-globalization activists who had been galvanized by protests in Genoa and Seattle under the banner of "another world is possible" converged on the city that year and would do so for the next four years. In total, hundreds of thousands of international activists participated in the forum's events. Hundreds of workshops and presentations on participatory budgeting took place, and several international networks dedicated to local participatory democracy were formed and convened at the forum.[48] Several PB "pioneers" in Europe and North America actually credit their visit to Porto Alegre during the World Social Forum, and learning about PB, as the first inspiration for their initiatives. Many of the activists who convened in Porto Alegre that year understood participatory budgeting as part of a renewed leftist project, one that overcame the historical limits of authoritarian and bureaucratic socialism. PB also showed that leftists could govern well, succeed electorally, and offer a compelling alternative to technocratic good governance based, as they had been doing over the last decade, on social justice principles.

While development agencies were looking for new alternatives to top-down structural adjustment programs, leftist activists were looking for successful and democratic alternatives to state socialism. Their struggle against global economic institutions underlined their search for new political organizations and institutions that could defeat "new public management" administrations. Alter-globalization activists were looking for other modes of governing in a pragmatic sense. They hoped to base these modes on affirmative proposals instead of "just protesting against the world-wide injustices, inequalities and disasters created by the excesses of capitalism" by "working towards creating a practical and theoretical framework for a new kind of globalization."[49] For them participatory budgeting was the "key to the success" of the Workers' Party's new and effective kind of governance. The party's PB process had become a "symbol" and a "social laboratory" for the left's possibilities and for a "new, developing democracy."[50]

Both the World Bank-sponsored event and the World Social Forum show how the Workers' Party had enrolled substantively different subjects around PB: an institutional and bureaucratic agent focused on administrative efficiency, and a critical grassroots imaginary focused on social justice principles and other practices of good governance. With its success proven in Brazil, Porto Alegre's participatory budgeting began to travel internationally as a success story of "good governance." The idea was attractive on the left and the right because the Workers' Party had separated PB from local social movement influence *and* associated it with a transparent and efficient administration. Yet the process of translation from one context to another turned PB into an instrument abstracted from a political project altogether, one associated with the neutral idea of "good governance." One more element had yet to be removed before it could truly travel globally: administrative reforms.

Traveling the World and International Toolkits

In November 2001 Porto Alegre's mayor, Raul Pont, and head of planning, Ubiratan de Souza, were invited for a series of talks in southern Spain to promote participatory budgeting. They timed their appearance in Córdoba to coincide with the symbolic ending of that city's first year of PB, when citizen delegates handed the mayor their list of one hundred chosen projects. The next day Porto Alegre's representatives gave talks to a packed audience made up of social movements and participants in that year's process. This was followed by closed-door meetings with city officials and implementers.

The meetings were so full that participants were turned away, and in the confusion they wound up running late. There were occasional difficulties with communication across Portuguese and Spanish. Nonetheless those present would later describe the meetings as "profoundly inspirational" and "transformative." At both events the Porto Alegre delegation received the kind of celebrity treatment reserved for celebrities, not city officials and planners from a medium-sized South American municipality.

Perhaps the most striking element of the trip were the public presentations, in particular those of de Souza, the director of planning in Porto Alegre. Of course most attendees were thrilled and proud to share their modest experiences with the radical administrators from the Global South. But de Souza's talk was free of leftist platitudes or utopian gestures. In fact he was highly technical and down-to-earth, focusing on the "how" and not the "what" or "why" of participatory democracy, as one attendee recalled. His presentation, at times in bureaucratic tones, followed the steps of composing a yearly budget, allocating it to departments, and coordinating between them. Rather than invite participants to dream of a just society, the talk explained how to reconcile efficient administration, open participation, and the implementation of policies based on social justice. As Mayor Pont would say later, this was the utopia of reconciling apparently opposing ideas.

The talk in Córdoba was emblematic of the way Porto Alegre officials framed their project at the time and typical of the international presentations: a series of slides that connected rational efficiency and social justice in a dense, sixty-minute speech. Several of the slides were concerned with the mundane details of the various administrative reforms, such as property tax increases, the reassignment of technical staff, and most of all the creation of a new planning department. But as the experiment began to spread beyond Latin America and Spain, this part of the talk became increasingly less prominent. And as others began to translate Porto Alegre's story into a set of applicable lessons, it dropped out altogether.

The globally replicable version of participatory budgeting and its best practices had no elements of administrative reform, and PB was essentially reduced to a set of meetings. At this time practitioners distilled it into a set of easily adaptable procedures and documented these recommendations in local or regional implementation manuals. These documents served as guides for other projects, typically framed as "toolkits" rather than "blueprints."[51] The toolkits' uniformity is notable.[52] Versions produced by different organizations (such as the UNDP or the World Bank) reveal very little substantive difference between each other, even between toolkits that came out of the World Social Forum and development organizations. Most provide a step-by-step methodological manual outlining each stage of the implementation process. They sketch the process from its original design (dividing the municipality into geographical regions, deciding the rules, etc.) through to the monitoring stage. The toolkits offer advice for government officials carrying out the process, such as expected challenges, recommended content for citizen manuals, and trainings for government employees involved in the process. Toolkits highlight the universalizing ("giving voice to all"), rational, and transparent procedures of PB that transform the wishes of the grass roots into sensible, quantifiable, and comparable demands. The promised results are tangible and desirable for either international agencies or the grass roots: better distribution of public money, and citizens showing a greater concern for public well-being. These results thus lead to practical benefits like increased tax revenues, and larger successes like solidarity among the population. Everyone wins: politicians prove their legitimacy and strengthen their popularity; citizens gain civic virtues; administrations gain capacity.

The content *absent* from these toolkits is also striking: they completely neglect Porto Alegre's administrative reforms that fell outside of the strict boundaries of "participatory budgeting" meetings. Tool-kits present PB as an isolated device that practitioners can make compatible with many different kinds of administrations and in various contexts. In toolkits the success of participatory budgeting depends on the willingness of the administration (politicians and civil servants) and citizens' civic efforts. Decoupled from the state, PB maintains visible similarities as it is translated from context to context, but the less visible arrangements of connections change considerably. As such the visible elements—meetings, rules, and the yearly cycle—can be rendered compatible with the most diverse administrative projects.

There are innumerable examples of PB's adaptability. In the 2000s in Venezuela, for example, *both* USAID and internationalist activists of the Chávez government promoted PB (Venezuela also adopted it as a national policy). In England, the PB Unit, a nonprofit consultancy dedicated to promoting participatory budgeting, describes in one of its how-to pages how to pitch PB to your local city councilor. The how-to instructs advocates to choose from a range of arguments based on the particular councilor's political leanings. PB's local empowerment emphasis resonates with greens and progressives, but centrists and conservatives are also drawn to its model; they see it as a *"sensible* step in decentralising and localising responsibility." In this way PB is promoted as fostering "community cohesion," "innovation," "social entrepreneurship," and "restoring trust" in government.[53]

The globalization of PB has been something extraordinary. As we have mentioned, after Brazil's successes with PB, local administrations in the region (Argentina, Chile, Uruguay, Peru, Ecuador, Colombia, Venezuela, Guatemala, the Dominican Republic) beginning in the mid-1990s developed dozens of municipal participatory budgets, while in Peru and the Dominican Republic PB became a national policy.

Europe was the first continent beyond South America to adopt PB. Progressive European politicians saw possibilities for PB within the context of ongoing discussions about political disaffection and lack of political legitimacy. European cities began to implement this idea in 2001, which Giovanni Allegretti and Carsten Herzberg described as the "return of the *Caravels.*"[34] Administrations in the south of Europe (Spain, Italy, and France) established the first European examples of PB between 2001 and 2005. These initiatives can be directly attributed to the influence of the World Social Forum, from which many leftist politicians at local levels in Europe imported an instrument that promised to face disaffection with participation and a tested method to support administration.

Simultaneously public administrations throughout the continent were experimenting with ways to bring the citizenry closer to the government as we have described in Chapter 2. Between 2000 and 2010 European PB experiences increased from a handful to more than two hundred. At this point their presence in Northern Europe began to exceed their counterparts in Southern Europe. In 2015 Britain was planning two hundred PB projects; Germany anticipated over one hundred; and the new left Portugal national government was planning the first ever national PB in the world. Participatory budgeting is held in small and large towns or cities: from Figaró in Spain and Borbona in Italy (with one thousand inhabitants), to Cologne, Edinburgh, Madrid, and Paris. Some experiences link the process of PB with concrete spaces of decision making open to all inhabitants. Others follow a "consultative" model in which the public meetings are sites where citizens can express complaints, needs, and hopes within a mechanism of "selective listening." In this model elected officials make the final decision on spending priorities. The methods used across these sites are also diverse: from the selection of participants by means of lottery (random selection), to the participation of association or NGO representatives only, to open and general participation (as in most cases).[55]

The diversity of PB attempts speaks to implementers' inventiveness and the role that different local actors have played in cobbling together their PB experiences. But it also speaks to the plasticity of

PB as an instrument, a plasticity resulting from its apparent political neutrality and low institutional profile. A commonality in European cases is that the vast majority of cases require no institutional reforms or changes.[56]

Development projects brought PB to Asia and Africa in the mid-2000s. The World Bank's involvement in these projects helped propel PB to Africa, usually in partnership with NGOs and other development agencies. The first experiences were in Cameroon, where a local NGO in partnership with the World Bank-funded Municipal Development Partnership and UN-Habitat organized a conference on the participatory process. In 2004 these organizations signed a letter of intent for the promotion of PB in Africa, which signaled the beginning of a large PB effort on the continent. This endeavor would come to include several workshops, training manuals, a radio show, and an online component all aimed at African countries. The letter facilitated dozens of experiments in most African countries by the late 2000s.

Participatory budgeting expanded into Asia slightly later and with less of a coordinated strategy. A series of direct exchanges between city governments, development organizations, and global NGOs resulted in PB's spread throughout Asian countries. UN-Habitat or the World Bank sometimes sponsored these efforts or they followed exchanges between international actors. In 2004 the South Korean and Brazilian municipalities worked together to establish PB, and in 2005 China and Brazil collaborated in an effort to set up PB throughout China.[57] Participatory budgeting is found today in cities in Japan, South Korea, China, India, Indonesia, and Thailand. In 2009 a German foundation within the orbit of the Social Democratic Party (the Friedrich Ebert Foundation) along with the Marc Bloch Center (Berlin) and Zhejiang University in China promoted the first Asian-European Congress on PB in the city of Hangzhou in China.

As we describe in Chapter 5, PB decisively arrived in North America in 2009, the first cases being in Chicago's Rogers Park neighborhood, followed by New York City, and then Vallejo in California. These followed on some previous experimentation in Canada, including the Public Housing Agency in Toronto and a short-lived attempt in Montreal. Somewhat closer to some of the European experiences, the U.S. cases were first developed around small discretionary budgets available to individual city councilors.

The overall numbers of PB's spread are impressive. By 2005 there were roughly 200 PB projects outside of Brazil; by 2008 there were at least 500; and by 2010, the sum total of PB experiments was at least 1,500. The estimates for 2015 were that there were at least 2,000 ongoing PB processes, including a dozen in the United States.[58] In less than fifteen years PB has turned itself into a global instrument, connected to ideas of good governance, detached from a political project, and disconnected from administrative reforms.

Landings: Democracy in Motion

In light of the nuances and contradictions of PB's evolution across the globe, the initial puzzle with which we opened this chapter—the World Bank and the Tenants and Workers United's similar interest in PB—should seem less surprising. The story of course confirms the general idea that policies "move in bits and pieces—as selective discourses, inchoate ideas, and synthesized models," rather than as complete and coherent blueprints.[59] But more specifically we can connect PB's broad draw to two aspects of its translation into a best practice: its progovernance appeal, and its separation from other, broader administrative reforms.

Participatory budgeting's main appeal is that it is a tool that can improve governance. It has become one of many tools available that constitute good governance. PB satisfies the criteria of "things that enable a government to deliver services to its people efficiently," made possible by a "combination of transparent and accountable institutions, strong skills and competence, and a fundamental willingness to do the right thing."[60] It is seen as something that can yield greater accountability and give voice to citizens in public decision-making processes, improving good governance from outside of the administrative machinery. Like many other tools for good governance, it is prized for its value-neutrality, the ease of its implementation, and its ability to attract many kinds of institutional stakeholders.

In other words policy makers today call for PB when there is a deficit in good governance. Otherwise PB experiments would be redundant, as a World Bank expert on participatory budgeting argues: "If there is a democratic process, participation, if there is rule of law, then Participatory Budgeting is not needed." Only in the absence of democratic participation, "*then* one has to have some sort of participatory process to hear the voices that have not been heard."[61]

Yet the global, best-practice version of participatory budgeting has been decoupled from the administrative reforms and from the machinery of the state. By not defining participation as part of the administration but *as an external tool that can influence it*, it became much easier to implement. Thus even if local governments across continents adopted the idea of PB and maintained the structure of meetings, the institutional architecture that linked those meetings to the centers of influential decision making was invisible.

If PB traveled in the 1990s as a centerpiece of a political strategy, as a standard-bearer for a new kind of electoral left-wing politics, in the 2000s it traveled isolated from the comprehensive administrative reforms that linked it to the original political project in Porto Alegre. This made it a more malleable tool, compatible with any number of political projects. Another clear consequence of this transformation is the marginalization of social justice principles that inspired the initiative in the first place. In this way participatory budgeting, as a politically polyvalent method to improve governance from *outside*, first became an attractive idea in both Europe and the United States. It arrived in this detached form in two cities that became emblematic cases of participatory budgeting: Córdoba in Spain, where it was carried out from 2001 to 2007, and Chicago's 49th Ward, where PB first landed in 2009 before being emulated across the rest of the United States.

In both Spain (and Europe more broadly) and the United States there was a public debate on the failings of these democracies in the years preceding the introduction of participatory budgeting. In 1999 for example when the administrators of the city of Córdoba began to discuss the idea of participatory budgeting, wider public discussions in Spain were attempting to understand disaffection with the country's democracy some twenty-five years after the end of the Franco dictatorship.

The global expansion of PB shows us the way in which democratic innovations gain presence in administrative projects throughout the world. Here democratic innovations do not seem to challenge any political narrative; as a matter of fact they fit well into contemporary contexts. However, as we will explore in the following chapters, the process of adaptation to local contexts unveils conflicts and political strategies that reveal the difficulties of expanding new ways of ruling without reshaping the citizenry's imagination.

Local implementations of participatory budgeting can be highly variable. In the next chapters we take up this question by looking more closely at the two emblematic "landings" of the idea in the United States and Spain. As we noted above, instruments like participatory budgeting do not "land from heaven." When they do land they represent a diversity of interests and groups of actors interested in (or opposed to) the device, which carries with it a variety of impacts.[62] Understanding how the idea of PB landed in these two specific places, and how this arrival revealed ambiguities and conflicts, offers insights into the concrete mechanisms of translation and ultimately the emancipatory possibilities of this kind of participation.

CHAPTER FOUR

The Rhetoric of Emancipation: Córdoba, Spain

[Before participatory budgeting,] citizens were mimicking the workings of merely representative democracy. I believe we must not just regenerate, but actually bring in new people and new ways of behaving.

—Maria José Moruno, architect of Córdoba's PB[1]

The office of the Federation of Neighborhood Associations of Córdoba, in Andalusia, Spain, is on the second floor of a nondescript building that also serves as a municipal library in the industrial outskirts of the city, far from the medieval mosque and other tourist destinations in this midsized town's center. To an outsider the federation offices might look like a municipal department office, complete with computer monitors, cubicles, and institutional Formica furniture. Throughout the business day, people stream in and out to resolve problems, denounce government malfunctioning, and make appointments with federation officers. But it is not a government office—far from it. The federation is the representative body of the city's one hundred neighborhood associations. These associations have for at least the last four decades played a number of roles in their neighborhoods, from organizing social events and hosting bullfighting-watching parties to mutual assistance and being an organized voice before government. As longtime activists will repeat with pride, active neighborhood movements like Córdoba's played a pivotal role in challenging the highly centralized nature of the Franco regime.[2]

The similarity with public offices is also not entirely accidental, however. The federation is an officially recognized body before city government, receiving direct funding from city hall through subventions and generally playing an important role in the city's political life. Its representatives even sit on the administrative boards of public companies.

In 1999 it was the federation that organized a series of working groups on participatory budgeting, the novel idea from Brazil. The year before, a leftist coalition headed by a faction of the former Communist Party, the Izquierda Unida (IU), had won city hall after a four-year hiatus for the left, and the victory brought with it a lot of hope for change. Córdoba became the largest city in Spain ruled by the IU at the time, with many of the elected city councilors complete outsiders to the dominant two-party political system that structured Spanish politics. One of those newly elected city councilors was Maria José Moruno, a schoolteacher and veteran of the city's feminist movement, who had the idea in 1999 to promote PB in the town and had reached out to the federation for assistance.

The federation, as part of its working group, invited the Porto Alegre practitioners to Córdoba in late 1999. Shortly after, Moruno sent a government colleague to the first World Social Forum in Porto Alegre in January 2001 on a fact-finding mission. She also began a dialog with a group of academics from Complutense University in Madrid, led at that time by an expert in participatory methodologies, Tomás Rodríguez Villasante. Villasante had been teaching the case of Porto Alegre in his graduate courses, and a number of his students had been doing research on it. For the federation participatory budgeting was a natural extension of its larger efforts to encourage citizen participation in the city and a natural evolution from its current role in the city's public decisions. For Moruno, because she was an outsider to political parties and associations, the attraction was that participatory budgeting would play a democratizing role in civic life, breaking with Córdoba's traditional practices, which is why Porto Alegre was such an inspiration for her.[3] The city of Córdoba did indeed launch the process the next year in 2001. It was one of the first European cities to launch PB, arguably the first "large city of the Old Continent" to do so.[4] In practice however Córdoba's PB project turned out to be more complicated than either Moruno imagined or the federation originally anticipated. Moruno encountered several obstacles as she attempted to implement participatory budgeting. From the inception her efforts faced resistance, and participatory budgeting was marked by a sense of experimentation and unpredictability. Over its first two years in particular, participants in the process came to clash with both city technocrats and organized neighborhood associations.

The City of Córdoba

This would not be the first time that Córdoba was an innovator in progressive urban politics. Since its first democratic elections in 1979 Córdoba had continuously been recognized as a leading city for participatory innovations, such as its model of permanent "district councils." Located in the region of Andalusia on the banks of the Guadalquivir River, Córdoba has a population of 300,000 and is one of the poorest large cities in Spain. It has historically relied on tourism and handicrafts, and its residents have struggled with chronic unemployment for the last several decades. Despite the fact that the Conservative Party has always had strong popular support here, it has only held power twice in the city's history. For many years it was the largest city in Spain ruled by the United Left. The mix of well-entrenched conservative traditions, the left's influence on city politics, citizens' desire for participatory innovation, and economic difficulties constitute the political context in Córdoba.

Local democracy, as mentioned, had been an important part of political life in Spain since before its transition to democracy. Contemporary neighborhood associations appeared in cities like Córdoba in the late 1960s, making demands for democratic decision making around the "the urban question."[5] Under the influence of leftist political thinking and progressive Catholic doctrines, neighborhood associations fostered community life, made concrete demands of local administrations, and demanded citizen participation. Once democracy arrived in 1975, those movements became important agents in the defense of education, the right to housing, and other social rights. As in Brazil, the social movements communicated their programs to the political parties, especially those on the left.

The idea of participation was central to these associations and already in 1979, with the first communist mayor in Córdoba,[6] an early effort was made to debate the public budgets with the citizenry. This did not last long but it shows the impetus democracy was gaining in those early years in Spain and in Córdoba particularly. In 1981 Córdoba associations then helped develop the Statute of Citizen Participation, one of the first in Spain, which created a series of councils to have a voice in city affairs, including fourteen district councils with representatives of associations, cultural groups, and parent-teacher groups meeting on a regular basis with representatives of the local administration.[7] Today, inspired in part by Córdoba, most medium-sized and large cities in Spain have similar statutes that stipulate councils, where associations are invited for dialogs with the person who has political responsibility for a determinate public sector—what Joan Font has described as "democracy of councils."[8] Since the 1980s the city has also had a municipal department dedicated to promoting citizen participation, and has developed a series of public boards that run its public utilities. Yet despite the fact that neighborhood associations had an estimated forty thousand members in the early 2000s,[9] there was a growing sentiment that the citizen movement and its model was running out of steam despite its impressive achievements in creating channels of communication with the municipality.

Creating a "space of equals"

Although Moruno was able to convince the mayor and the rest of the councilors to develop a participatory budgeting process, there were constraints from the mayor's office from the start. A first condition was that Moruno herself lead the process. In addition the city did not provide her with resources for significant infrastructure projects as had been the case in Porto Alegre, which had inspired her. The process would use a much smaller budgetary set-aside and level of support than Moruno imagined. The administration dedicated a pool of roughly three million euros ($3.6 million) from its budget and allowed her limited staff support. The city also approached the Complutense University of Madrid for technical expertise and enlisted one scholar who specialized in participatory methodologies to assist the city with the technical coordination of the participatory process.

Moruno was, significantly, an outsider to the political mainstream, which in the city of Córdoba included organized neighborhood associations. In her view currently practiced modes of participation and associational life had failed to revitalize politics and incorporate new voices; participatory budgeting was a potential solution that broke with the tired routines of civil society and city government. Moruno reflected on her experience years later: "I believe that participation was [at that time] reflecting the habits of purely representative democracy. . . . I thought we should welcome fresh approaches and new modes of behavior." In this context Moruno imagined PB as part of a struggle to conquer new spaces. She remembered, "[I] used to say that PB was a plant we were watering, and many will want to cut down this plant; but as long as we can protect its roots, we can succeed."

While PB was part of a long-term vision to enhance democracy, she had to take more immediate steps to attempt to successfully institutionalize it. She continuously emphasized the rhetoric of PB as a "space of equals" in order to present the process as politically neutral and widely accessible. She constantly referenced this equality as a way to question the organization of civil society and the bureaucratic and elitist perspectives underlying the structure of formal political representation.

In early January 2001 city facilitators held citizen assemblies in each of the city's civic centers, conveniently located in each of the fourteen districts. Although the city government developed the PB's overall outlines (infrastructure investments, universal participation, and a yearly cycle), some key procedures like the actual decision-making process were still to be decided. This open scenario was in line with the proposal for participation brought to the city by Villasante, in that participants decide the structure and then rethink it every year. It would be up to the residents elected at those first assemblies to define the final form of the process: whether to hold neighborhood assemblies, how to involve the general public, what voting procedures to use, whether to use criteria to prioritize certain projects, and how to coordinate with neighborhood associations.

At those first assemblies facilitators described the purpose of participatory budgeting and explained how citizen decision making on budgetary affairs would enhance democratic participation in the city. Attendees then chose a total of eighty-seven representatives who would decide on the specifics of the process and take the next steps. These representatives, called *agentes* (from *agentes comunitários*, or community agents), received more specific training in February, including on budgetary and technical issues relating to infrastructure investments. They also began to make decisions about the rules for the process.

The issue that caused the most consternation for the *agentes* was how to relate the participatory budget to existing neighborhood associations. Although most *agentes* were themselves from associations, they did not have clear agreement about how to articulate the direct participation through the assemblies and the representative forms of associations. Some thought associations should direct the whole process, while others thought associations should have no role in it. In the end it was decided to create a "district roundtable" in each district, in which representatives of associations and *agentes* could establish guidelines for who would run and coordinate the next stages of the process. This division of labor was codified in the *autorreglamento*, a book of rules that would be revisited every year by participants. The city's material repeatedly referred to this as a form of "coresponsibility."

In March the city council sent postcard invitations to all residents' homes and advertised on local media the times and locations of a series of neighborhood assemblies, roughly three for each district. The *agentes* rather than the municipal staff (although with support from Moruno's office) again explained PB at these forty-three assemblies and facilitated discussions in the neighborhoods. Residents who participated in the neighborhood assemblies could propose ideas but did not vote on them. Participants proposed projects and prioritized criteria. For example after the neighborhood assemblies a facilitator might leave with an unranked list of a dozen ideas for projects, such as a children's playground, a library extension, or a soccer field, as well as a ranking of criteria, such as (1) social justice, (2) environmental sustainability, (3) economic development, and so on.

A district assembly then followed in April and May, where both the *agentes* and the representatives of neighborhood associations discussed the prioritized list of proposals, also applying the agreed-on criteria. "Social justice" was the primary criterion in Córdoba in those first years. The result of these assemblies then was a list of ranked projects, which was to be passed to a final "city roundtable." To everyone's disappointment no city officials participated in these district meetings.

Finally a citywide assembly took place in June, in which two *agentes* from each of the fourteen districts decided among all of the ranked proposals, again applying the chosen criteria. Before the meeting Moruno's department suggested that the *agentes* ride the bus together to visit sites of potential projects, an idea inspired by the Porto Alegre process. During the bus ride the district representatives had the opportunity to defend their particular projects and address questions. The technicians responsible for city hall's finances and infrastructure then sat down with the *agentes* from each district, explaining the technical problems of each of the proposals. Some *agentes* withdrew their proposals because of anticipated complications. After a marathon day on the third Saturday of September, the *agentes* made their decisions. As in previous assemblies participants did not vote directly but evaluated projects on the basis of criteria on a scale of one to three. A few days later, in October, all the *agentes* offered the proposals to the mayor of the city, Rosa Aguilar, in a ceremony in the city council. It was the first contact between the mayor's office and the public after nearly a year of participatory budgeting. All told, in PB's first year about three thousand residents of Córdoba participated. Organized associations, general participants, and city officials managed to carry out a process that maintained a fragile equilibrium between them. Yet as the novelty wore off, the balance would not hold for much longer and actors began to push back against the new process.

Holding the Line

One of the largest sources of resistance to the PB process actually came from within the administration itself, from the ranks of the city's bureaucracy. In February 2002 the director general of the presidency of the city of Córdoba, the highest bureaucratic authority, had to call a meeting to define city management's strategy in the participatory budgeting experiment. After a year, facilitators assigned to PB had begun to demand resources from the administration, while technical staff were often put in difficult situations as they experienced a transformation of the nature of their work. The technical experts are responsible for explaining why the administration has rejected certain citizens' proposals. And of course they must respond to citizens' concerns and allow them to feel as if they have some power over meetings' agendas. Every time participants inquired about the record of decisions made during the previous year, for example, these municipal officers had to carry out research, and they would complain to their superiors about these "new" responsibilities. And as the administration expanded requirements for what would constitute viable projects, the workload for city engineers and experts expanded accordingly. By the end of the first year the process involved a large and growing number of municipal employees in different areas of management. As the second year of the process began, critical voices within the administration began to vigorously contest both the workload and citizen encroachment on their expert terrain.

Over the course of the first year *agentes* in Córdoba had stepped into the work of governance. They debated priorities and delved deeply into seemingly mundane issues. In so doing they acted in spheres normally occupied by city bureaucrats. The process of rank-ordering projects, for example, generated intense conflicts within the administration, which was accustomed to deference on these issues. The engineers, city planners, and career technocrats believed that their experience working on municipal projects accorded them a certain degree of authority.

The tension between *agentes*, who claimed a voice through the new process, and the city bureaucrats, who were suspicious about these new dynamics, grew over the first year. To avoid conflict going forward, this necessitated an external and authoritative figure to make final decisions. Moruno attended the meeting but there was a great deal of suspicion toward her from bureaucrats, so the director general with the help of an external consultant ran the meeting and adjudicated between Moruno and the rebellious bureaucracy. The city, the director general stated at the opening, was deeply grateful for the PB project and considered it a great success. After all, three thousand people had taken part in over one hundred assemblies, and all had offered opinions and learned about the functioning of the municipality. However, as the meeting went on and he fielded complaints from bureaucrat after bureaucrat, he eventually offered a blunt statement. The goal of participatory budgeting, he argued, "is to promote the budget proposals," while participation "is a secondary effect." He clarified as he went on that "the budget is the end and participation the means, the instrument, not vice-versa."

The statement clearly reflected how officials viewed PB as a potential threat to the established bureaucratic order. In his view citizens have needs that guide the decisions of the bureaucrats, who are simply neutral intermediaries. PB serves one of the many mechanisms of gathering input, but "participation" in and of itself is of no added value, if not a directly destabilizing influence. But now, and in contrast to the past, newly empowered citizens were constantly demanding elected politicians' involvement in the process. Municipal employees echoed the director's wishes in calling for a more neutral process free of these sorts of influence. From then on the director and others in the higher echelons of the administration sought to demarcate a line of separation between the inside and the outside, between civil society as an informal schematic structure, and the administration, including political parties, as a formal structure. Administrators must continuously work to maintain this division. In short, the director emphasized that there must be a separation of "the formal structures from the informal structure (participatory budgeting)." He conceded that some day "[we] will inevitably articulate them," but for the present "they should function as parallel structures."

It seemed impossible to reconcile the emancipatory rhetoric of participatory budgeting, as propagated by Moruno and the *agentes*, with the neutral rhetoric of the administration. For their part *agentes* and other participants insisted on the political dimension of their experience, demanding more and more say over technical matters and more accountability from the bureaucracy. One of the controversial issues in the second year was whether city officials should attend assemblies. After the first year, *agentes* began to demand their attendance to provide information and qualify the discussions. But they were met with refusal time and again. As one city official put it at the time, "Our technical staff works within the administration" while "assemblies are outside of it." He went on to explain that "assemblies are made up of citizens; technical staff do not have anything to do there." Other excuses for not attending meetings included what seemed to *agentes* like obscure definitions about skills and difficult and complex administrative demands.

The local government from that time established a line between the administration and the participatory process. City officials gave several reasons for this division. Sometimes they cited the complexity of the technical architecture; other times they noted the inability to address the demands for legal reasons never made explicit. Sometimes they referred to guiding principles ("to work for the city as a whole" or "political priorities") that structured the budget, displacing citizens' priorities into a secondary space. Sometimes they simply declared that "participatory budgeting is not the same as the legislature." From the bureaucracy's point of view, dealing with participatory budgeting required an ongoing effort to maintain a precarious balance. Officials had to negotiate between safeguarding political representatives from changing their way of doing politics while trying to appease citizens who believed that participatory budgeting meant doing things differently.

In a response to a group of *agentes* about city decision making in 2002, for example, the director of the city of Córdoba explained: "The budget is done by items, rather than projects, and then politicians decide what is included. It may be that part of the infrastructure budget has no projects, but that money is in another part of the government team, so perhaps the project that you demand is not in the area of infrastructure and maybe they [those responsible for infrastructure] do not know it. If you knew the inner workings of City Hall, you would see that sometimes it is not possible to give all information." In Córdoba other officials in addition to the director sought to avoid the internal spread of a new style of governance. They actively sought to neutralize participatory spaces and their influence within the administration, minimizing what they described as PB's "collateral damage" of opening up too many spaces to citizens.

By the second year of the process most of the municipal staff responsible for facilitating the PB process in the neighborhoods of Córdoba were actively resisting its implementation, as were all of the upper municipal bureaucracy. But reasons and arguments were different. The staff that dealt directly with participants were aware that the PB instrument bolstered citizens' expectations, but they did not think the process implied additional accountability on their part and wanted to reserve a space for expert decision-making power over proposals. The upper-level echelon, on the other hand, was much more concerned about filling the pipeline with unqualified proposals and ideas. There were periodic training courses for city staff in departments like finance and infrastructure that would be involved in PB processes. These trainings were usually a site of friction and airing of grievances. It was not unusual at these for city staff to complain about the dangers of participation and discuss ways of managing citizen expectations. At one training the director of the education department, with a career spanning more than thirty years in public service, after hearing several of these complaints, explained the source of the problems to her newer colleagues. She articulated that citizens usually behave within a "consumerist" mentality: "They are unable to think of the city; they propose many self-interested [projects] and this can be a disaster." Technical staff perceived the public's lack of information and igno-rance as hindrances to legitimate participation. PB "beautifully opens spaces to the public," she paused, before advising, "[but] we cannot do everything they say."

Associations against Lay Citizens in Córdoba

If the bureaucracy pushed back against the dangers of participation, the greatest conflict that arose was actually between participants and members of organized neighborhood associations. As we have men-tioned, in Córdoba neighborhood associations have been the tradi-tional channel of communication between the population and the government, including a number of councils playing an advisory role in city administration. And although associations had been one of the protagonists in bringing PB to Córdoba in the first place, they quickly changed positions and began to see PB as a threat to their standing. Most upsetting of all was the city's emphasis on "one person, one vote." This new model of organizing representation around individual citizens caused many association representatives to resist and openly criticize the participatory budgeting effort from its inception, eventu-ally leading to its demise.

Moruno had actually been quite aware of the associations' strength and potential opposition to the process before launching it. After the visits from the Porto Alegre delegation in 1999, it was clear this was going to be a problem. The visitors insisted on the importance of the principle of individual (and not associational) participation, some-thing that had not been quite as clear to association activists before-hand. To Moruno this was actually one of its attractive features and she understood it might cause consternation if not handled delicately.

She kept in contact with sympathetic association activists through-out the planning stages and in late 2000 called a meeting for all of Córdoba's association leaders and activists. She hoped to neutralize their negative reactions and avoid a rumored boycott of the first assemblies. In a tense meeting Moruno tried to convince the civil society representatives that PB was intended to remedy the decline in citizen participation and could actually come to strengthen associations. She explained: "The PB is not against associations; all of you can participate. But we should consider that people are increasingly less involved and if we get more people to participate, certainly they will also participate in associations." She also argued that association leaders could be involved in the organization of PB's procedures if they were elected to public assemblies. From this position they could actually monitor the process from within. The meeting was a relative success in placating nerves.

The participatory budget began in earnest in January with a number of hopeful signs. The associations did not call for a boycott of the meetings, and some actually worked to publicize the first assemblies. Nearly two-thirds of participants at the assemblies came from neighborhood associations, and seventy of the eighty-seven elected *agentes* held some elected position within neighborhood associations in the city. While there was some open grumbling from some association leaders who desired a more formal role for associations, Moruno and her allies considered this first round a resounding success given that 20 percent of the *agentes* were not affiliated with associations.

Associations played a prominent role the first year. When *agentes* were assembled to decide on the rules of the process, they gave neighborhood associations in the various districts some responsibilities for organizing assemblies. Participants from neighborhood associations played a prominent role in each district. And all but four of the final twenty-eight participants in the "city roundtable" charged with deciding the final list of projects were from neighborhood associations. Nonetheless association leaders continued to demand that the PB process recognize their unique role and felt Moruno and her allies had intentionally sidelined associations.

As the process started its second year and it seemed it would be organized along the same principles as the year before, leaders of associations stepped up their public criticisms. They took to the local press claiming the participatory budgeting process intentionally marginalized associations and their long history of fighting for Córdoba's communities. The main demand was that the PB project include a formal role for associations so that their representatives could address grievances, hold PB leaders accountable, and advocate for citizens' needs. Several associations, including those represented by the Federation of Neighborhood Associations, boycotted the process in its second year. As a result of this pressure, citizen participation in the process decreased by one-third in the second year and it would never again reach its original numbers. Associations also started to pressure city government directly to either dismantle the process or open a parallel channel for associations. Moruno resigned that year because, she said, it was no longer possible to carry out the political principles that had led her to government.

On the face of it the opposition to participatory budgeting by the associations is paradoxical. Neighborhood associations are a fundamental part of the fabric of civil society in the city, and many of them have long histories dating back to the struggle against the dictatorship. They are voluntary associations committed to community empowerment and citizen access to government. Their concern with "council democracy" was precisely that it was not participatory enough. So why did they oppose a system of open citizen engagement around the budget that would allow their members to make decisions on public investments?

Activists with neighborhood associations fundamentally rejected the concept of a new public sphere that would restructure how city issues were discussed. In particular they rejected open participation by the nonassociated. First, they worried it would foster a kind of *individualistic* participation. The president of the Federation of Neighborhood Associations in Córdoba asserted at the time that "an individual who is not in an association will be unable to act in solidarity with others . . . . A person acting on his own behalf may contribute in a neighborhood meeting, but probably the only thing he'll do is resolve a personal and individual problem."

A second common refrain had to do with the historical role of neighborhood associations. As one representative of a neighborhood associations complained: "We are obligated to participate as any other citizen, when I've been involved in the association twenty-five years. This is not right." These two common arguments implied that unorganized individuals are unqualified for participatory democracy owing to their lack of political skills. Another activist with neighborhood associations commented that citizens "need to have a mandate, be instructed, know the minimum rules of town planning, the regulations and the laws, and be able to speak. In short, they ought to have a certain set of qualities." Implicit is the idea that those in power would be able to easily manipulate these unqualified citizen participants. Therefore familiarity with political parties and their mode of operating, which Moruno perceived as a weakness of associations, was actually understood as a strength.

Those aligned with associations felt PB would weaken their countervailing power and fail to acknowledge the value of their collective knowledge. They questioned structuring public opinion through open procedures and felt that government uses them, along with deliberative practices, to neutralize this countervailing power. For them, changing the political system in this way signified a diminishing of democracy; the president of the Federation of Neighborhood Associations expressed that PB was an "operation that democratizes the public debate, but which also destabilizes the traditional associations."[10] They further criticized participatory budgeting for "preventing us from attacking the core problems: how the city was financed, what state model was desired."

The government suddenly had an oversized problem. If PB had been a campaign promise, it was also supposed to be a minor program and not a source of visible conflicts. This provoked ambivalence in the government, which was manifest through indefinition in its participatory politics. In those years it was not uncommon for the administration to hold meetings with associations in parallel to participatory budgeting meetings. In April 2003 for example a PB assembly was held in Levante, one of the city's districts. Simultaneously, in the same civic center building but in a room located on a different floor, the mayor along with city hall staff met with neighborhood association representatives to talk about possible infrastructure investments in the district. In the back office, when the director of town planning was asked by some *agentes* about the parallel meeting, he tried to justify the government's political position on the basis of legitimacy. Proposals would be chosen from "three sources: electoral proposals, participatory budgeting and private meetings with neighborhood associations, all of them legitimate for the government." Emboldened with statements like these, associations began to apply even more pressure on the government to dissolve the PB experiment.

After the 2003 elections the new municipal administration, also from the Izquierda Unida, decided to heed the demands of associations, now framing it as a way to "resolve many of the experiment's contradictions." One of the contradictions, according to the new administration, was that participatory budgeting proposals could sometimes be inconsistent with the party's political platform. The process was modified to include a veto point giving city government the final say on accepting or rejecting participants' proposals.

The associations' persistent opposition to PB and the passive attitude of government against the critics mobilized the *agentes* to defend it. In 2003 a group of them created the "Citizens' Platform in Defense of Participatory Budgeting." As one of the *agentes* recalled, "We believed that the model being used [for participatory budgeting] had many defects, but one good point was one person, one vote." Some eighty *agentes* wrote and signed a manifesto that they sent to the media and to city government. The manifesto read in part that "one person, one vote is what guarantees democracy and participation of all citizens." The platform mobilized several hundred former participants, took out ads in the newspapers, and lobbied members of city council.

These *agentes* took up a position in sharp contrast to that of the neighborhood associations. For them the political space opened up by PB created a vital opportunity to participate in city politics. They felt that PB broke down obstacles to participation, and they strongly defended the process's deliberative practices as well as the universal subject of participation. These new participants' conception of politics prioritized deliberation over protest or representation. PB allowed them to debate and reach the best possible decisions about city affairs. Because PB departed from a predefined set of questions, the process enabled a sense of shared responsibility. In doing so it incorporated new voices into the political process. These new participants described PB as a political process in which citizens could play a role in city politics while also learning the intricacies of government operations, where one "could learn many roles."

Importantly for many participants in PB it was also an opportunity to democratize neighborhood associations themselves and more generally a tool to enrich local democratic life beyond the stalemate of associational life. One recalled that "when you put associations together with non-organized citizens, it was very enriching. They were generous and showed solidarity." This was not an antiassociation position, but they argued that the associations' claims of expert knowledge hindered other citizens' efforts to participate in the political sphere.

Despite the pressure from these *agentes*, in 2005 the city conceded to the demands of the associations. The city council decided to dramatically transform the process by favoring the associations' complaints over lay citizens' support, changing the rules, and increasing the formal role of associations around budget proposals. From then on, participatory budgeting became what was later referred to as a "mixed model," with some direct participation and some participation by neighborhood associations, which now had a set number of seats in the district and city roundtables. One of the results of the reform was that it actually decreased the number of participants in 2005 and 2006. In 2007 the process was quietly shut down without protest.

Making Sense of the Conflicts in Córdoba

Ultimately participatory budgeting in Córdoba presented a political dilemma over how to legitimize public decisions. Neighborhood associations interpreted PB as a depoliticizing mechanism. If citizens had to decide on proposals in a context of limited resources, it could "set one neighborhood against another,"[11] instead of challenging the lack of resources in the first place. Associations claimed that traditional politics required representatives who rule and make decisions. It was these representatives' responsibility to monitor the political agenda and oversee its implementation. After these decisions were made, citizens would elect the most effective politicians. In this view PB would complicate this system. If PB were implemented in neighborhoods, those associations argued, political representatives would lose their responsibility.

But for proponents of PB like Moruno this new process signified the opposite: in her vision it would repoliticize the public space. Moruno was willing to delegate some of her electoral power to others. This required setting up a different set of rules, which would sacrifice old ways of doing politics and invite participants to make proposals.

In light of the persistent criticisms against individual political participation, one *agente* tried to justify this new participatory logic in his neighborhood assembly: "I know that at assemblies citizens will ask many things depending on individual interest, and maybe it's not the best for the district. But the point of this process is collective learning. If we don't make mistakes, if people do not make a mistake, it is impossible to learn and do well." PB created a political process that allowed lay citizens to get involved in community affairs, make decisions about particular issues, and then see the consequences of these decisions. In this way the "common good" did not conform to a preconceived idea but referred to a reflective and ongoing process.

Faced with this "romantic" idea of the common good, representatives of the neighborhood associations movement in Córdoba wanted to link the PB process more closely to associations. As the president of the Federation of Neighborhood Associations expressed, "That's [in associations] where you learn to look around the neighborhood, the city, where you have to think for everyone, not just for yourself." In contrast, he argued, "[because] participatory budgets are based on individual participation, that vision of the common good is impossible; there is no solidarity." Their way to meet the challenge of individual and direct participation was not only to radically oppose this process but to offer the government a new participatory structure.

This new structure, the "mixed model" we describe above, was inspired by the "more pragmatic" idea of the common good and solidarity. Before participatory budgeting, neighborhood associations, through representation in the "Council of Citizens Movement," were the only partners with the government at the city level. Now they proposed to extend the "Council" with the representation of other associative sectors, creating a new "Municipal Regulation of Citizen Participation." Moruno's vision and the associations' resistance to it demonstrate the clash of two radically different approaches to politics.

In Córdoba the government also tried to maintain its power. When associations pressed for changing the participatory budgeting protocols, the government took advantage of their opposition to insert a new rule to condition the results and monitor proposals coming from below. All proposals would in advance fit within the political program of government. Thus the city government held on to the ultimate decision-making power to accept or reject citizen proposals.

The Córdoba Model and the Spanish Participatory Wave

In the case of Córdoba the transformation of the original PB into a "mixed model" facilitated the project's collapse and the story ended in seeming ignominy for the main parties. Nonetheless by that time Córdoba had become a national and international attraction as an exemplar of participation in Spain and Europe and as an important model of participatory budgeting.[12]

In its first years, between 2001 and 2003, Córdoba was the great promoter of the new participatory experiences in Spain. At that time representatives from many cities throughout the country passed through Córdoba's town hall to hear about lessons learned. In fact the basic PowerPoint slides that Córdoba' mayor used in his public presentations were only slightly changed by city officials in other towns in their own presentations. The slides that dealt with internal coordination of municipal departments, training courses for city staff, participatory methodologies at the assemblies, and the cycle of meetings were reused in several other places, and this accounts for some of the identical features of those processes. The city of Córdoba also invested resources in international promotion, coming to join and eventually host activities of the URB-AL Network-9. As we discussed in Chapter 3, this was an important node of exchange between cities of Latin America and Europe.

Starting in 2004, as Córdoba transitioned to the "mixed model," Seville, Getafe, San Sebastian, and Jeréz de la Frontera implemented participatory experiences based on the Córdoba template. Córdoba's success in implementing a process and its difficulties with neighborhood associations were important in the shaping of these subsequent processes. They each imitated several features exactly—such as the format of meetings and the role of city experts—and they each began processes with negotiations in mind for organized associations. The city of Seville, for example, the fourth-largest Spanish city (700,000 inhabitants), built on Córdoba's scheme, and there was an intensive application of the participatory methodologies, also advised by the Madrid-based group of scholars that had advised Córdoba. The yearly schedule and the format of the process, including its structure of delegation, came from Córdoba. And even though the process was led by the same left-wing party (the IU) that had led the process in Córdoba, conflict with civil society was never quite the issue in Seville that it was in Córdoba. Associations were in a sense placated from the very beginning. Organized associations had a role from the very beginning of the process and had a number of seats set aside at the various roundtables. The process in Seville lasted several years longer than Córdoba's, and Seville came to take the mantle as the city leading participatory budgeting in Spain and Southern Europe.

Córdoba's legacy goes much beyond that. Despite the ostensible failures and conflicts we described, it is curious how these events are remembered from the point of view of those involved in participatory budgeting in Córdoba. Even if the government was to reduce the impact of participatory budgeting in the administration, its implementation in the first place had generated a series of expectations, some of which had to be met. The newly opened space of participatory budgeting (deliberative and inclusive) empowered participants to claim a distinct relationship with the administration, one that was more transparent, less hierarchical, and based on mutual respect. Still, in every conflicting moment the administration pulled the bureaucracy to its side, always attempting to relegate participation to a secondary level.

On the other hand, for the first time the associations had to face a scenario in which they were forced to justify their refusal of participation in the same space, while thinking about politics in old terms, focusing on the representatives, and moving the role that any citizen might have to a marginal position.

This is how the experiment is remembered—as an insurgent attempt to radically democratize city administration and an asymmetric struggle for sovereignty between a new political subject and a recalcitrant administration, on one side, and between that subject and ossified associations on the other. Despite the conflicts and ultimately the defeat of that subject, no one in Europe had gone so far. Scholars looking comparatively at participatory budgeting have labeled it the "European Porto Alegre" for its effort at including principles of social justice as a decision-making criterion, for the intense deliberative procedures, and for the attempt to bring municipal government under the mandate of inclusive, participatory spaces without hierarchies.[13] In 2014 the original model of Córdoba was still an object of analysis by academics highlighting the transformative potential of its methods with respect to other European experiences, even if at the end it had limited outcomes.[14] Córdoba became a symbol of the insurgent possibilities of participation within governance structures.

Córdoba's successes and failures also prompted an important debate in Spain about the purposes of new mechanisms of participation, which were being implemented in various domains beginning in the mid-2000s. If after Córdoba participation passed from being an unrealizable idea to a pragmatic possibility, it also acquired an important political valence: participation could be conflictive and about creating political spaces among equals directly related to governance.

It is possible to speak of a "participatory wave" in Spain, starting in the mid-2000s. By 2009 there were around one hundred participatory budgeting experiences in Spain, roughly half of them with hired professionals trained in any of the masters programs on participatory methodologies that had been used in the Córdoba and Seville experiences.[15] For a decade Spain was able to train a new generation of professionals aimed at managing participatory processes (not only participatory budgets), always characterized by deliberative tools, the inclusion of all citizens, and collective decision making. When the *indignados* emerged in the streets of Spanish cities in 2011, nearly everyone was surprised by their dynamics of discussion, but most had been taught and practiced in these participatory methodologies.[16] The demands of the *indignados*—transparency, political spaces without hierarchies, the inclusion of all citizens, participation as insurgency, and submitting governance mechanisms to participatory processes— have their roots in this very generation of participatory practitioners. Without fail participatory budgets were continuously referenced in *indignado* programs and policy ideas.

The outcome of the protests, as is well known, was the formation of new political parties with the capacity to bring policy changes to institutions. In January 2014 the new party Podemos emerged with a proparticipatory discourse, as did several loosely associated municipal platforms. In municipal elections in 2015 these won in several cities, including Madrid and Barcelona and many other cities. A large portion of the newly elected officials from these parties and the staff that work with them received their political education within this participatory wave. The current chief of staff in the city of Madrid for example was one of the external consultants hired by the city of Córdoba in framing participatory budgets in the early 2000s. The implementation of participatory budgeting in Madrid under this new administration will call on some of the same people who developed it in Córdoba.

From 2000 in Córdoba to 2015 in Madrid—a city under the rule of political forces that emerged among the *indignados*—it is possible to see continuities as well as changes in what participation can mean.

Today participation in Madrid is framed as transformative, something quite beyond some of the ideas of participation as management (as a "partition of the sensible") or even of bringing government closer to the citizenry. There is also now talk about calling into question just what is "sensible" and putting fundamental governmental and societal questions up for debate.

The current head of participatory initiatives in Madrid is Pablo Soto, who describes his political awakening with the *indignados* of 2011. A computer hacker who had previously achieved notoriety for his legal troubles around file sharing, he has put into place two "complementary" exercises, according to him, which address the participatory question differently. On the one hand, there are participatory budgets with which "citizens can directly choose small infrastructures" in their neighborhood or district. On the other, there is a forum for proposals and debates in which any citizen can intervene or propose any question. If any of the proposals reach 1 percent support from the Madrid population, the administration will hold binding referenda. If a referendum is approved, the government will carry it out, "independently of whether the mayor and city council do or do not agree." For Soto this effort at "revolutionizing democracy" reflects the evolution of participation to a next logical level. It is also an effort to "appropriate a power the elites have had in direct form."[17]

CHAPTER FIVE

A Government Closer to the People: Chicago, Illinois*

Tucked in an alley behind the Rogers Park "L" stop—Chicago-speak for metro station—the Glenwood Bar is hardly the type of neighborhood institution that makes history. Yet at four o'clock on April 10, 2010, Joe Moore, surrounded by his staff and bleary-eyed from counting votes, approached a microphone, faced a film camera, and declared: "We, in the 49th Ward, for the first time in the history of the United States, have turned the decision making over city dollars to you, in the first ever participatory budgeting process." Although his audience was intimately familiar with this unprecedented story, Alderman Moore recounted how over the past several months residents had developed several projects that the ward's infrastructure budget could fund, and then voted on them. As alderman his only duty was to report the results of their vote: twelve projects, including the ward's first dog park and a community garden. The audience celebrated the announcement of each winning project with shouts and cheers. It was an evening of accomplishment: for the winning projects, the 1,700 people who had voted on them, the dozens of volunteers devoted to the process, and the project's one organizational staff person. Perhaps most of all the evening was a victory for the alderman, an elected official who had "brought democracy" to the community surrounding the Glenwood. Though celebrated like any other neighborhood event,

*This chapter is authored with Nicole Summers.

this party marked the official arrival of participatory budgeting on American shores. The 49th Ward's ability to implement PB demonstrated that this methodology for direct citizen decision making on public budgets could work in the United States.

Chicago's 49th Ward is a long way from Porto Alegre, but it was the first port of call for participatory budgeting in the United States. Although it was a circumspect experiment, it played a crucial role in the adoption and replication of the experience elsewhere. Chicago's PB was the model for New York's, started two years later, and in Vallejo, California, a year after that, providing the template for the dozen or so experiences in the country at the time of this writing. PB even received mention in the U.S. federal government in President Barack Obama's Second Transparency Plan. For many observers Chicago's PB was a harbinger of possibilities for democratizing current structures and bringing government closer to citizens. The Penn Medal of Democracy, which was awarded to the Participatory Budgeting Project, described PB as "*the* most important democratic innovation of the 21st Century."

Politely avoided in that first evening of celebration, however, was a controversy that had been developing over the role of the "Steering Committee." The steering committee, a group of community activists appointed by the alderman to oversee the process, had come under some criticism from other participants. The controversy finally boiled to the surface in an "evaluation meeting" held two weeks later. Many issues came up at the meeting but none as heated as the charges brought against the steering committee: devoted participants who were not members alleged that the committee was essentially made up of friends of the alderman who exerted undue influence on a process that was supposed to be about direct democracy. Steering committee members, for their part, felt stung by the criticisms after having done the lion's share of work to get the process started—from designing the rules to facilitating workshops. After an acrimonious series of exchanges that lasted into the next days, the alderman stepped in, dissolved the steering committee, and formed a new "Leadership Committee" made up of former steering committee members and some of the dissenting participants. Although the issue was settled, emotions continued to run high over who "owned" the process, especially as it was then later emulated elsewhere.

Like Córdoba's participatory budgeting experience, described in the preceding chapter, and like Porto Alegre's in Chapter 3, Chicago's nascent participatory budgeting was shaped by controversies that surfaced at its inception and by the eventual resolutions to these controversies. If Porto Alegre's participatory budget in the 1990s was part of a broad politico-institutional project to transform the local state, and Córdoba's in the 2000s was imagined as a "space of equals" that might confront entrenched bureaucracies and staid neighborhood associations, the goals in Chicago nearly a decade later were much more modest and less confrontational. Here, and much more in line with contemporary concerns of the "new spirit of government," the goal was to bring government closer to citizens, to fight apathy, and to strengthen community. It was also an institutionally more modest proposal. Unlike in Córdoba, city agencies and staff were hardly involved in the process, except at a few crucial moments of approving projects. By and large the process took place *outside* of the government machinery, with outside expertise and dependent on volunteers. The money set aside for it—discretionary funds available to each alderman and intended for small infrastructure projects like street resurfacing—had never been on anyone's radar as an object of political pressure. Still, several significant controversies surfaced over its first year. These came to the fore on issues over technical expertise, on what constitutes good citizenship, and on who was most entitled to speak for the process.

From Machine Politics to "Happy Talk" in Rogers Park

The city of Chicago has a well-known tradition of machine politics, charismatic politicians, and entrenched corruption. The city is also

home to pockets of grassroots activism represented by aldermen independent of the machine. The 49th Ward is known for the latter.
The 49th Ward ("Rogers Park") is a diverse and economically mixed
lakefront area (population 60,000) at Chicago's North End, ten miles
north of downtown and abutting Evanston. Once a predominantly
white neighborhood, in more recent times scholars have described
it as "self-consciously diverse."[1] That is, the ward is a neighborhood
where residents publicly repeat and value "diversity discourse."[2] Yet
for some this discourse only represents a variant of "happy talk" that
avoids difficult topics and reproduces whiteness.[3] Indeed the racial
composition of Rogers Park matches Chicago as a whole. Unlike most
neighborhoods that are dominated by one or two groups, Rogers Park
is roughly 10 percent Asian, with whites, African Americans, and La-
tinos each having a proportion close to 30 percent of the population.

Rogers Park is very much known in the city for its liberal politics.
It currently boasts a high number of neighborhood associations and
community-based projects and is well known for a number of very
active political bloggers.[4] Rogers Park achieved acclaim in the past for
its community policing), art spaces like the Mess Hall, and affordable housing organizations fashioned in the style of Saul Alinsky, as
well as community organizing more generally. These liberal politics
have always had an uneasy coexistence with a range of conflicts over
the neighborhood's future, particularly around its economic development.[5] Until the 1970s it was considered a "stable" white neighborhood; but since its demographics began to change, the lines of conflict
emerged between white homeowners' associations and groups that organized low-income tenants.[6]

Moore was elected 49th Ward alderman for the first time in 1991.
A lawyer and former activist with the local Democratic Party organization, Moore has been reelected five times by carefully balancing
different interests in the neighborhood. He is nationally known for
advocacy of liberal causes like the infamous municipal law banning

foie gras (eventually repealed), and for taking symbolic stances on the invasion of Iraq. A founder of Cities for Progress, Moore also fought for a "Big Box Living Wage Ordinance" in the mid-2000s as well as for more comprehensive recycling. On the other hand, he has been criticized in the neighborhood for worrying about issues that will get national coverage at the expense of neighborhood concerns. Others have criticized him for a "project-by-project" practice of decision making and for the lack of transparency in neighborhood development and destination of tax increment financing (TIF) funds. As Ellen Berrey writes, "There is no elected board to formulate a broader neighborhood plan or convene periodic public forums," and Moore's "redevelopment task forces and committees almost always consist of white, affluent organizational leaders and homeowners," only acceding to low-income housing proposals when under pressure.[7]

Participatory democracy at the ward level had some precedent in Chicago prior to Moore's introduction of participatory budgeting. In the 1970s for example 44th Ward alderman Dick Simpson created a "Ward Assembly" to direct all of his decisions including his votes in city council, a form of direct democracy emerging from social movements of the time. Alderman Moore's decision to introduce participatory budgeting to the 49th Ward in the summer of 2009 was nonetheless quite novel. His constituency had not demanded more opportunities to participate in local politics. Moore had learned about participatory budgeting at the 2007 U.S. Social Forum and through his connections with Cities for Progress, a national network of progressive city officials. He was excited by the idea of implementing a process that would be the first of its kind in the United States. Knowing his activist constituency, he also believed the community would receive the project well. The possibility that this experiment could score him badly needed political points after his previous election—which he won in a close runoff as a third-time incumbent—was a convenient by-product, according to his public statements on the subject.

He contacted the Participatory Budget Project, a nascent network of volunteer experts interested in implementing PB in North America, and the group provided him with guidance based on experiences elsewhere.[8] Moore's stated goal, however, as he described it at public events was to put power back into the hands of "the people" who had given it to him in the first place. This goal became complicated throughout the process as the PB "recipients" asserted different ideas about what it meant to give power to the people.

The First-Year Process

In the 49th Ward, Moore used PB to allocate his discretionary "menu money," a $1.3 million fund given annually to aldermen for infrastructure projects. The fund is a trivial matter in Chicago city politics; constituents are largely unaware of it and allocation decisions face little public scrutiny. Thus when Moore proposed participatory budgeting for the 49th Ward, not only was the process of deliberation foreign to residents; the community was unfamiliar with the budget itself. From the start Moore recognized that he faced an inherent contradiction in trying to build a bottom-up process from the top down. Early on he convened a steering committee of local activists to put a "Rogers Park stamp" on the process. With help from the Participatory Budgeting Project the committee made initial decisions regarding the design of the process (writing and approving a rule book), met regularly to plan its next steps, and facilitated the first community meetings. Throughout, the steering committee thought of itself as the backbone and directive body of PB in the ward.

In early November 2009 the PB organizers held nine neighborhood assemblies throughout the ward—eight in different neighborhood areas and one wardwide assembly for Spanish-speaking residents. After the steering committee sent out invitations and e-mails to presumably all thirty thousand households in the ward, residents turned out in small but substantial numbers; about forty community members attended each initial meeting. The assemblies were divided into two main parts. First, the alderman and the steering committee introduced the concept of participatory budgeting and the details of the menu money budget. The facilitators explained that the project aimed to transfer power to the people in the spirit of a more "democratic democracy." They also provided information about some of the constraints and common uses of menu money. In the second part of the meeting, participants were divided into discussion groups to deliberate about infrastructure needs and priorities. Participants proposed a range of ideas such as a community swimming pool, pothole filling, murals, and bike lanes. Steering committee members facilitated these groups, operating as if they knew more about the menu money budget than the other participants. They believed this meeting structure would ensure that the initial stages of the process ran smoothly. At the end of these initial assemblies the facilitators invited residents to stay involved in the process by becoming community representatives. These "Community Reps" as they came to be known were responsible for developing concrete spending proposals for the final wardwide vote.

About sixty residents volunteered to become community reps. Each rep chose to serve on one of six budgeting committees: transportation, traffic safety, public safety, parks and environment, streets, and art and other projects. Committees met separately and could exercise considerable discretion in determining the process, outcomes, and criteria for project selection. There was no minimum or maximum limit to the number of projects that could be slated; members could work in subcommittees or together as one group; and whether decisions would be based on community needs or on representatives' interests was open for debate. Ultimately the six committees proposed a total of thirty-six projects ranging from street resurfacing to bike lanes to community gardens.

The PB facilitators then placed the proposals, including project descriptions and estimated price tags, on a ballot. They invited all ward residents age sixteen and over to vote for up to eight projects—a rule the steering committee developed before the process began. Community reps and the steering committee organized a massive "get out the vote" effort involving yard signs, community banners, and displays of project posters. Many community representatives campaigned for their committee's projects. Over the course of a single voting-day event and a week of early voting, over 1,600 people cast their ballots in a ward of approximately 30,000 eligible voters. The projects that won the most votes were funded from the $1.3 million of the alderman's discretionary budget.

Experts vs. Citizens

In between the genesis of the idea of participatory budgeting in the ward and Joe Moore's success in concluding the projects, there was a year of messy politics; contestations and controversy abounded as the process was developed. One of the main recurring set of conflicts, as in Córdoba, involved questions of expertise.

In Chicago the "transportation committee" was the site of one of the most active groups of community reps. This committee, composed of about fifteen members, drew a mix of activists demanding increased bikeways on the streets, recreational bikers and walkers who wanted more pathways along the lake, and individuals motivated by a general concern for the community and improved transportation. The committee met twice a month as a full committee and also broke into various subcommittees (such as a "sidewalks committee"), some of which met separately. One of the issues the transportation committee addressed early on was the perceived lack of usable and safe bike lanes in the ward. Committee members repeatedly expressed concern about the need to find a way to "separate bikes from cars on the street." The committee searched for creative, innovative solutions to the problem. It researched other cities' models and members were surprised to uncover a range of alternative biking infrastructure models already in use. Excited by the possibilities, they developed a project proposal based on a combination of features from these existing designs. Their proposal involved a wide stretch of bike lanes that would be separated from the streets by an additional curb that would divide biking and car traffic. "Curb shifting," as the structure is widely known, is already used in several cities recognized for their bike friendliness, such as Portland and Paris.

In every way, the community reps' particular style of local innovation was in line with current decentralized governance philosophy: they wanted to develop an ambitious and sustainable bike lane project based on best practices but tailored to local needs. Yet the project still needed the city's blessing in the form of a feasibility approval before it could be placed on the ballot. In theory this should have been a minor step in the process.

Once the community reps had developed their idea for the project, they arranged for a meeting with the City of Chicago Bicycle Program. The meeting was held in the evening at Rogers Park after weeks of preparation on the part of the reps. They felt confident about the project's goal—segregated bike lanes—and also had collected detailed information about cost and regulations from city planners. The representative from the city, a planner in his mid-twenties from CDOT (Chicago Department of Transportation), arrived at the meeting with his standard presentation in hand. He began by giving an overview of the CDOT Bicycle Program and followed with a PowerPoint presentation of the city's bikeways programming. The latter involved a description of the typical bike lane design, which all of the representatives were more than familiar with: lanes separated by painted lines on streets that met certain width requirements. To the community reps present, the presentation was uninformative and elementary, if not downright insulting.

The community reps had also prepared their own PowerPoint presentation on their project. They explained the curb-shifting design they wanted to propose, outlined how and why they thought it could work, and gave a brief overview of the implementation schemes in other cities. The CDOT planner, surprised by the presentation, responded by dismissing their ideas as "creative but infeasible." Curb-divided bike lanes would have to be at least ten feet wide, he said, because city snowplows have a ten-foot clearance. Lanes of that size were cost prohibitive, not to mention unsuitable for most streets. For this reason Chicago was limited to designated bike lanes and a few other options. Curb-shifted lanes simply could not receive feasibility approval, he said. The representatives were frustrated and disappointed and the meeting ended in chaos.

Over the next weeks the committee continued to contest the merit of the city planner's assessment. Rather than accept and adapt to the logic of the planner, they argued that he was making a technical issue out of something that was in fact political. The city requirements, in the words of one rep, were "chosen policies, not naturally imposed limitations." The representatives also resented being shut out of the debate. Though they were not professional technocrats, engineers, or planners, they were nevertheless citizens. As residents of the city and affected recipients of its policies, they felt entitled to a legitimate voice and influence over city planning. On another level the representatives felt that the city officials' claims to superior authority over policy decision making were unjustified because their "expert knowledge" was shallow. The bikeways planner had asserted that curb-shifted bike lanes were infeasible, yet cities around the world had implemented them. The representatives saw a clear way around the snowplow issue and proposed it as an alternative: buy smaller plows and then build smaller bike lanes. One representative asked if it "had occurred to anyone that maybe we could build a five-to-six-foot-wide bike lane . . .

and buy Bobcat snowplows?" He also noted that it could clearly be done, because "[the city] already clears the bike paths."

The city did not relent from its judgment, however. Despite repeated pleas by community reps, CDOT did not deviate from its original position. The transportation committee then became embroiled in its own controversy: should it accept the watered-down version of bike lanes on the street, or should it not submit a bike lane proposal at all? Was it worse to capitulate to the bureaucratic mandate or to have no new bike lanes? For some of the younger activists committed to a "postcarbon lifestyle," capitulation was seen as treason to the greater cause. For others who adopted a more "pragmatic" stance, a watered-down proposal still represented progress because it would lead to greater awareness about biking and might lead to better bike lanes in the future. A difficult compromise position eventually emerged: the restricted bike project would go on the ballot under the subtitle "Phase 1," thus signaling future expectations. Some of the activists left the participatory budgeting process at this point. But all agreed that the city's explanation reflected not expertise but rather bureaucratic impotence and stifled creativity. One representative further noted: "Somehow Chicago can't [build curb-shifted bike lanes] because we need ten-foot-wide bike lanes, and no one has thought about how the snowplow idea is just, goofy. . . . So we're not looking at something the rest of the world is doing for a stupid idea that there's a very easy way around."

A similar controversy erupted over a project to build a dog park, or a dog-friendly area (DFA). The DFA project emerged within the parks and environment committee, which drew neighborhood professionals and environmental activists. For years residents had demanded a DFA and some became involved expressly for this purpose. Early on in the process community reps settled on the idea of the dog park at Pottawatomie Park, in the center of the ward, and then submitted the project idea to the alderman's office, which passed it on to the city for a price estimate.

The Chicago Park District (CPD) has a fixed price of $150,000 for the conversion of parks into dog-friendly areas. In response to the community reps' request for more information about the price, the CPD said it was based on the cost of adding new features to the park, such as a fence, water fountain, and bench, which were required for qualification as a DFA. At first the community reps criticized the requirements themselves. They simply wanted the DFA designation, which would allow dogs to run off-leash, and did not see why they should also have to pay for what they saw as unnecessary features such as a fountain and bench. The requirements seemed arbitrary and disconnected from any sort of public will. Because the park district cast the terms as "requirements," so the criticism went, they were shielded from subjection to democratic contestation. Quite simply the CPD presented the DFA requirements as "technical" despite their irrelevance to the engineering of a dog park, and nonnegotiable despite their inherently political nature.

Finding technical requirements a non-starter with the park district, the community reps then called into question the validity of the CPD officials' claims to expert knowledge on pricing. Even with everything included, $150,000 seemed incredibly high to them. One of the community reps, a landscape architect who had been awarded contracts from the city for similar sorts of projects, performed a price estimate as if he were bidding for the contract. Even with upward estimations of all costs—unionized labor, expensive materials, etc.—he projected costs slightly over $40,000. The representatives confronted the CPD with these numbers and asked for an explanation of the difference. The CPD provided none. At best, the city officials said, they could drop the price to $110,000, but they would need to eliminate most of the extra features from the design. Of course to community reps this seemed hypocritical: the proposed "compromise" directly contradicted the CPD's previous statements; what was once nonnegotiable was now being negotiated. Community reps remained dissatisfied and attempted to enlist Alderman Moore's help. They persisted over the following weeks in questioning the city about the price, but the CPD was firm in its refusal to provide details or to move on the price. Pricing had always fallen within their arena of expertise and hence authority, and they felt no obligation to meet new accountability standards imposed by people with no explicit authority. The dog park appeared on the ballot anyway, at the price of $110,000, but the process generated discontentment and distrust of the seemingly arbitrary technical vetting process of the city.

The several months of debate and controversy over these two projects resulted in these participants questioning the politicization of technical criteria. Community reps on both the bike lane and DFA projects recognized that engineers and city planners had a role to play in the development of sound infrastructure policy, but came to feel that these experts had overstepped that role. They also felt the city used "expertise" to justify the insulation of policy decisions. The city had always based decisions like these on internal technical expertise not subject to outside scrutiny. The halls of the Chicago Department of Transportation and the Chicago Park District were filled with city planners, engineers, and career bureaucrats whose jobs were to determine the parameters for infrastructure development. They defined what sorts of projects fit within these parameters. The ward offices were simply supposed to choose from among the predetermined sets of options. In short, city officials believed there was a definite line beyond which there was no room for politics or the citizen mandate. In their view some realms of decision making belonged to experts, not citizens.

More intriguing than the bureaucratic logic of the city's planners is how participants in the process resisted what has been described elsewhere as the "rule of experts" or "expert closure."[9] For the most part participants came to see "feasibility" as a mask for the political priorities of other existing governance bodies. Thus, as the process unfolded, rather than acquiescing to the logic of governmental expertise, the PB process constantly challenged the status quo. Instead of molding communities to align with the priorities of government institutions, PB generated significant friction around the priorities themselves. If city agencies viewed expertise as definitive, specific, and authoritative, community reps considered it qualified and general, and informative rather than prescriptive.

These two projects and many others sparked intense debates over the function and standards for expertise-based authority in a democracy. In the 49th Ward, whenever participants interacted with "experts" they contested who decided the feasibility requirements, the specifications of these requirements, and their relative responsiveness to citizen input. The overnight rise to power of a new, distinguished class of citizens—the community reps—threatened agencies' power not only in a distributive sense but also by calling into question their claims to authority. At times citizens became unruly in their dealings with city bureaucrats. They contacted their offices directly without consulting with the alderman, which created tension between the PB facilitators and the local government. One participant even accosted a municipal department head on a Sunday when they were both at church. Some of the alderman's employees who liaised with municipal departments worried about these strained contacts; one employee felt "it was kind of weird to have a constituent contacting the assistant commissioner." Many participants frequently complained about the experts' role in the process. They appreciated learning about the city's rules and regulations, but they began to expect recognition as legitimate interlocutors. City bureaucrats resisted.

One committee member recalled that "we had a lot of contact with experts, and most of it face-to-face. . . . I can't say we were im-

pressed." In the 49th Ward the PB process also provoked contestations over the legitimacy of power within a democracy. Engaging in
city politics provoked several profound questions. For example does
"expertise" or instead citizenship lend itself to more legitimate claims
to speak for and on behalf of others? If expertise prevails, then what
constitutes an expert and to what extent does expertise trump politics?
If citizenship matters more, what values does "citizenship" demand of
the citizen? Both city experts' and citizen participants' views around
these questions did not necessarily predate these conflicts, at least not
in their fullest forms. Rather, interacting with the contested process of
PB had defined, refined, and crystalized their perspectives.

In the 49th Ward, after the first year of PB, the relationship between the city councilor's office and the city agencies was somewhat
formalized. Experts from city agencies played a more immediate role
in the process, vetting projects earlier. And they also reasserted their
technical authority. In no uncertain terms did these experts notify the
ward office that their technical vetoes were final and not up for discussion. Despite participants' attempts during the first year to transcend
the boundaries of the process by redefining some of the terms of engagement, the enduring version of the process was one in which technical expertise subordinated citizen knowledge. And notwithstanding
some early ideas of transcending the restrictions of menu money, or
allocating greater portions for infrastructure, or even seeking other
pots of money, the process remained tied to the small discretionary
infrastructure budget.

Competing Notions of the Good Citizen

In Chicago disputes between the ward office and the transportation
committee also represented the struggle over the definition of good
citizens. The 49th Ward's PB procedures allowed citizens to challenge
the alderman's staff. Instead of associations' representatives it was committee members and the alderman who determined the face of the

common good. Several representatives on the committee were interested in proposing a project for a bike path along the lakefront. Like many other projects the committee was considering, a member had suggested this at a neighborhood assembly and other participants were attracted to the project once they heard about it. The idea was for a paved path over sand to run directly alongside the beach, which would connect two existing bike paths that run north to south throughout the city. As the proposal moved forward, it demonstrated how new modes of representation can generate conflict. The committee proposed the path because participants wanted more recreational space for biking and walking. The proponents of the project were self-interested in the sense that their goal was to improve their own pursuits. To them this seemed like a legitimate motivation: they were residents of the ward and as such felt justified in making a demand they believed would advance their personal interests.

According to recollections by participants, the alderman's office did not agree. The staff recognized that the representatives were entitled to make demands as citizens in the process, but they held that *legitimate* demands were grounded in concerns for the larger community. Many residents, especially condominium owners whose land abutted the property, would oppose the path. Thus, as one participant remembered, the concern was raised that the committee "needed to think in terms of the whole neighborhood." They were told by the alderman's office that "we should have taken this opposition into consideration, and the fact that we did not was taken as disregard" for the community's wider set of interests. The bike path proponents' self-interested motivations conflicted with an unspoken assumption of good citizenship. It was not enough to want a project that would satisfy your own interests, however reasonable they may seem. Rather participants should want the project to benefit the entire community, and propose it in terms that reflected this interest. This committee did not frame its proposal in terms of the best interests of the ward or even certain factions within it. They also did not claim that the project advanced interests that were in any way separate or disjointed from their own. Because they framed their demands in this way, the alderman's office viewed them as less legitimate speakers for "the public." Speaking for the public meant speaking for the people as an "other" whose interests were distinct from one's own.

According to the rules, the alderman's office could not directly block a committee's proposal. However, it had tools to prevent it from moving forward. Participants usually expected the alderman and his staff to use their resources and connections to support the committees' projects. While the office fulfilled this expectation for most projects, this was not the case for the bike path proposal. Staff members with relevant background information refused to attend the transportation committee meetings; the office only reluctantly made necessary calls to city agencies; and technical support was inadequate. The alderman's office's response seemed disciplinary—it showed that "bad" citizenship would not be rewarded the same way as "good" citizenship. The project was thus removed from consideration through "foot dragging" in the words of one community rep. Some of the community reps were infuriated, seeing no reason why their motivations for the project would evoke these penalties. Others, who prided themselves in having no particular interests at stake in the process, sided with the alderman's office for "doing the right thing so that the whole community's interests are considered." Though the alderman's office attempted to exert control over the process, and did so "subtly" and "gradually," this did not result, as some of the more critical literature describes, in the transformation of citizens' demands and modes of thinking to align with those of the state. It did result in contestation that gave rise to new political actors, views, and relationships, which came to life throughout the process.

The Steering Committee in Chicago

Debate over the role of the "Steering Committee" was the central controversy that shaped the first year of participatory budgeting in Chicago's 49th Ward. Moore initially established the steering committee (SC) to ensure community buy-in and to provide a community-run counterpart to his office throughout the process. It was a priority, according to one participant, that "the process have Rogers Park's signature on it." In PB's early stages Moore sent out invitations to civic organizations in his ward—including schools, churches, block clubs, and social service agencies—to form a committee to help design and run the process. The first meeting was well attended. The organizations' representatives deliberated on and wrote the rules that would guide the ward's participatory budgeting experiment. They chose from a menu of options presented to them (such as "What should the minimum voting age be?") and made a number of important decisions regarding procedures and representation.

Early in the process some participants voiced suspicion about this "unelected group." One participant who had been invited to join the committee, a former opponent of the alderman in a previous election, skeptically questioned, "Is this just an extended circle of the Alderman's supporters and friends?" By the time the process itself was ready to launch, it was clear that participation in the steering committee was a significant commitment. It required attendance at many meetings, and members were expected to provide ongoing support. As the process unfolded, many committee members preferred to step back. Some representatives from social justice and service organizations articulated time commitment concerns; others asserted that the process did not directly serve the needs of their members who, as one said, "would not be concerned with sidewalks and dog parks." One community activist who left the process early on complained that "this was a group of professionals" and that "the Alderman is clearly not comfortable with working-class people." Whether the description is correct or not, the committee members who remained were civic minded and of a slightly older generation. The fifteen-member SC was made up of block club leaders, historical society representatives, park committee members, and members of a CDC (community development corporation).

As the process began, the SC evolved to serve several purposes. Members contributed time and resources in addition to lending the project legitimacy. Steering committee members decided on the format for the assemblies, advertised them, facilitated breakout groups, staffed informational tables, recruited volunteers, raised funds, and generally acted as representatives of the process for the ward. One of the early issues for the SC was who would introduce and emcee the neighborhood assemblies. The decision of the alderman's office to determine the agenda for the first assemblies and run the meetings caused strong resentment from SC members. They fired off hostile e-mails followed by a heated debate, until finally the alderman modified the agenda to include one SC member, who would introduce the assembly with the alderman. From the committee's point of view recognition of its role in the process was important. Some members put in twenty or more hours a week over several months. A member of the SC recalled: "It was like I had a second job. It was great, but it was a second job." Another described a sense of pride in having helped start the process: "[Participating in PB was] like giving birth to something that was totally new."

However, among fifty or so community reps that got involved with the process in the "second semester"—after the neighborhood assemblies concluded—suspicion was growing over the SC's role and legitimacy. At this point SC members held a bimonthly meeting with the alderman and his staff to oversee the process. Committee members had each chosen to participate in one of the issue subcommittees, deciding that they would play the role of mentor. The mentor would help clarify the rules or explain ambiguous points as well as directly connect with the alderman. In some of the subcommittees, for example, SC members argued in favor of some projects because of their presumed awareness of how this or that bureaucracy really worked. Sometimes they would provide the rationale for one of the alderman's decisions, based on "insider" information. Although they provided what they thought was an invaluable service, for some of the subcommittee participants they seemed to simply be a group of "unelected insiders" or "friends of Joe." For example as the final voting assembly neared and conversations about the effort to "Get Out the Vote" began, two artists on the "Art and Other Projects Committee" approached the alderman's office about designing an official flyer for the vote. Because up until that point the SC had organized these kinds of activities, the alderman's office turned the decision over to it. The SC said it would be open to looking at a sketch of the flyer. After discussing the flyer, though, members decided they wanted to be "consistent in the flyer graphics" and use the same design they had used for all previous meetings—a design by a member of the SC whose print shop donated all of the flyers. The two artists, who eventually dropped out of the PB project, felt dismissed and believed the design selection was unfair and lacked transparency. In subsequent conversations in the arts subcommittee the issue of the flyers came up again and again, some participants describing the SC as "a little shady" and accusing members of having "conflicts of interest" and "standing to benefit from their positions."

As the first year of the process was coming to a close, other problems with the steering committee rose to the surface. Some participants resented the mentoring in their subcommittees; others felt that an unelected body had no role in a participatory process. Many more were unclear about who was on the SC and what its mandate was. And as the process garnered media attention, frictions and jealousies arose about who would appear on camera. Moreover subtle tensions between SC members and subcommittee participants existed. As slightly older, civic-minded members of the community, SC members often had different styles from the younger, more "activisty" types who were on the transportation and arts subcommittees. For example SC members tended to be more respectful in their way of speaking of city officials or the alderman, whereas the younger activist types were more willing to use humor or more outrageous language to describe city bureaucrats. The "activist" group, raised on consensus meetings and political correctness, were much more concerned with respectful dialogue within meetings or the gender dynamics of a conversation. They were also much more familiar with tools used to run meetings—like listing action items and tabling items—and with operating technology. One subcommittee participant expressed with some frustration "that they [the SC] weren't even aware of what a brainstorming process was."

Two of the very active community reps, two young women who had been active in transportation and biking issues, were so troubled by the steering committee's actions that they approached the alderman's office about helping design the final evaluation of the process, which the alderman accepted. The evaluation took place in three parts: a survey at the voting assembly, a written evaluation for community reps, and a final evaluation meeting with all community reps and SC members.

The evaluation took place during a two-hour, highly organized meeting cofacilitated by two community reps and the alderman's staff person assigned to the PB project. Almost all of the community reps and SC members attended. The facilitators read comments from the feedback sheets, which ranged from mundane critiques about starting the process earlier, to sharply critical suggestions directed at the SC. Afterward the meeting moved to discussion in small groups. People were first instructed to sit with their subcommittees and discuss possible improvements to the process. Insights were posted around the room. Some of the suggestions included creating a governance body for the process that was open to all, detaching the process from the alderman's office and addressing feasibility issues sooner. Later in the meeting, participants would place dots next to ideas most appealing to them. The meeting had been quietly tense until it was announced that a "Process Advisory Committee" would form to go over the evaluation data and propose modifications to the process the following year. Some thirty people volunteered to join the "PAC" but as they did, steering committee members started to loudly complain. One member felt their role was being usurped (later describing this as "a coup attempt"); another demanded to know why the SC was not consulted about this agenda. The meeting erupted into a confrontation between the reps and the SC members, and ended in confusion.

The next day angry e-mails were exchanged. Several committee members felt insulted and betrayed. They felt that participants had disregarded their knowledge, experience, and expertise in running the process, and felt strongly that they should have been consulted about the evaluation process before the meeting. One member called the idea of the process advisory committee "just stupid." Many felt personally attacked and one member noted, "We felt that all of the hard work that we had put in was somewhat negated by the negativity." Another said that she was open to the younger activists taking charge but not with how they tried to do it. "They [the younger activists] took ownership, which is great . . . , but the way it was presented it made us feel like all of our hard work didn't mean much."

Alderman Moore promptly dissolved the process advisory committee. The steering committee and Alderman Moore met a few weeks later, at which point the alderman assured them that their experience and leadership in the process were valued and they were not being replaced. In response to the criticisms, though, Moore and the committee members decided to transform the SC into a "Leadership Committee," which would govern the process the following year. Though it was a decision made without the input of the community representatives, it seemed like a victory for the insurgent participants. A leadership committee made up of *any* interested former community reps and SC members would run the process the following year. Some thirty people volunteered to be on this committee at first; membership would dwindle, however, over the next months. By the time the process started again in the fall, the leadership committee comprised primarily former SC members. The precedent was set, and the implicit question the process posed was answered: the kind of practice that would be most valued—the way of speaking that would be considered most legitimate—was that represented by long-standing civic organizations. After the first year the leadership committee continued to play a very strong role in shaping the tenor of the process. Its "civic" orientation pervaded the process as a whole, and in many ways the 49th Ward's participatory budget would mirror its practices and style.

A few weeks later Moore wrote an e-mail blast to the whole community pledging continuity with the process; it was an "affirmation that people will participate in the civic affairs of their community if given real power to make real decisions." In the end, of course, controversies had been settled in ways that reinforced the power of city experts and the status of a founding group of community leaders. In an important sense the boundaries of the process became narrower in practice than at the start: expert rule extended over a broader swath of the process and community leaders with standing became even more important. The point is not so much the paradox that the process became narrower in the way that so-called empowering reforms can reinforce exclusionary citizenship, as scholars in many contexts have documented.[10] The point is that the boundaries were contested and settled over ambiguities implicit in the process itself.

The 49th Ward's process would not change significantly after that first year. There were, however, concerted though ultimately not very successful efforts at making the process more inclusive of low-income people of color in the ward's various neighborhoods. These efforts included raising money for outreach and identifying less traditional polling places like *bodegas* and schools to meet the "community where they are," in the words of one participant. And if the number of participants slumped in the second year, project implementation was generally successful and the process has continued on. By 2014 the ward completed its fifth cycle, managing to somewhat increase diversity in participation, produce ballots in several languages, and return to the level of participation and enthusiasm of the first year.

But if the process has struggled with inclusivity, the boundaries of the process have not expanded. No additional sources of funds have been added to the decision-making pool, and city experts are no more subservient now to the popular mandate than before. In fact the process has been tweaked so as to set aside more money for street resurfacing, one of the alderman's concerns, which has been interpreted by some as a narrowing of the scope of decision making. The main leaders of the project continue to be from the area's more traditional civic organizations and the Democratic Party, while the few others have faded out over time. Speaking of the overall PB process in Chicago, a group of researchers note that the leadership of the process comes from "neighborhood associations, block clubs, CDCs, arts groups, chambers of commerce, and park advisory councils."[11] Much less important are the kinds of youth practices connected to movements like Occupy, for example, or more social justice-oriented organizations that defend the rights of tenants and low-income residents of the ward. Occupy Rogers Park, for example, would stage a protest in 2013 against the 49th Ward's participatory budgeting process, accusing it of a lack of representativity, diversity, and democracy. And questions remain for some participants about the limits of the autonomy of the process and the alderman's outsized role in driving it. Rachel Weber, Thea Crum, and Eduardo Salinas describe the 49th Ward's process as being filled by a "top-down mobilization" strategy closely linked to the alderman's networks.[12]

The Making of a U.S. Model

Despite these questions the conclusion of that first year, and Moore's reelection, were important because participatory budgeting had passed its first trial in the United States and the elements of a successful "U.S. model" were emerging that would now be copied elsewhere in the United States. Moore played a very important role in helping diffuse the idea. In the fall of 2010 at a number of talks around the country he spoke about his success at several venues, including New York, Boston, and Providence, Rhode Island. Moore would several times credit his strong reelection in 2011 (in sharp contrast to the near-miss in 2008), when he won 72 percent of the vote, to the participatory budgeting process. He noted very openly that his voting margin went up by 42 percent since implementing PB, and that PB was "the single most popular initiative in [his] twenty years in the city council."[13] Participatory budgeting was also an object of discussion at the 2010 U.S. Social Forum in June of that year, and then featured at the meeting of the National League of Cities in December. Everywhere the argument was repeated that "giving power to the people," "bringing people closer to government," could also really "pay off" politically.[14]

In Chicago after the 49th Ward's second cycle other aldermen became interested in emulating the process. After some false starts, in 2012 the process decisively expanded to three other districts, now in a coordinated fashion and in partnership with a local institute and a nonprofit.[15]

The first city outside of Chicago to take up participatory budgeting was New York, starting in 2011, and this can be directly traced to Moore's success in Chicago. In sharp contrast to Chicago's process, here the process was partially driven by a community organization, one deeply rooted in social justice organizing and with a mission to empower underprivileged residents of New York City.[16] From the get-go, as its director stated, the goal was to foster "participation that represents the true diversity in which people live" and to make "special efforts to engage the populations that are often left out."[17] From the very first workshop on writing the rules in July 2011, the "New York signature on PB was inclusion," in the words of a participant. The second iteration of the rulebook emphasized "empowerment" as a key value, as have most of the promotional materials and the more vocal city councilors.[18] For example from the first year the rules stressed openness, and in some participating districts the voting age is as low as fourteen.[19] By 2015 half of the districts in New York had participatory budgeting, mobilizing thousands of participants, hundreds of volunteers, and involving dozens of community organizations in one way or another. The combination of the city's sheer size and its importance has made New York the marquee model of participatory budgeting in North America, and it has been the subject of several newspaper features, documentaries, and ongoing studies.[20] In September 2015 New York City's participatory budgeting process won the prestigious Ash Center Award for Democratic Innovation.

The city of Vallejo, California, whose process started in the fall of 2012, was the next place to emulate the process, which has been slightly less prominent than New York City's. Driven by a city councilor who was inspired by Chicago's process, this time the PB process was linked to a resolution calling for a new sales tax. A town of 120,000 in the outskirts of the Bay Area, Vallejo had undergone bankruptcy in 2008,[21] and those in government were willing to be "more innovative and risk-taking," which included the deployment of high-tech security cameras, greater use of Twitter and Facebook by city officials, and the introduction of participatory budgeting.[22] Voters approved a 1 percent sales tax increase ("Measure B") and dedicated 30 percent of those revenues to PB proceedings in what would be the United States' first citywide process. The initiative also included funds to hire a full-time staffer to run the process. A committee composed of a cross-section of Vallejo organizations put together a rulebook that emphasized the goal of "improving government," and it was open to participants as young as fourteen as well as the possibility of online project submission. In the third year the rules were revised to dedicate a portion of the budget program and service projects to "targeting the low-to-moderate income populations in Vallejo."[23] By all accounts, even though it is driven by the city council, the program is considered successful and popular with broad participation from different ethnic groups in Vallejo.[24]

By 2015 there were at least half a dozen functioning processes in the United States, including in Boston and St. Louis, and at least a dozen more in the planning stages. There is no doubt that participatory budgeting has arrived to stay in the United States. It has received mention in President Barack Obama's Open Government Plan and is mentioned by the U.S. Department of Housing and Urban Development as a best practice; further, the Participatory Budgeting Project won the prestigious Penn State Democracy Medal in 2014. In addition to processes directly assisted by the Participatory Budgeting Project, versions have been implemented by for-profit consultancies. The Participatory Budgeting Project itself, which originally assisted with the 49th Ward's process, grew into a formal organization and then into an incorporated nonprofit in 2011, and it has become the principal hub for PB activity in North America, being involved in dozens of processes or attempted ones, engaging publics as diverse as Occupy in New York City[25] or the White House Office of Innovation.

Most of the communities attempting PB in the United States at this time were following the Chicago model. In contrast to Córdoba's model, discussed in the previous chapter, these programs have largely had an overarching "civic" (rather than overtly "political") orientation, have been linked to very small administrative reforms, and have worked with small budgets for infrastructural projects over a yearly cycle. In the fall assemblies are held throughout the participating districts, where residents learn about the process and suggest ideas; delegates then take up the work in committees that vet and develop the ideas into projects. In the spring, sometime between March and May, a vote is held that is open to all residents. At some point before the next cycle participants have an opportunity to revisit the rules of the process.[26] By 2015 there was discussion of tapping additional sources of funding, such as TIF and the Community Development Block Grant program, and experimentation with online platforms.

With all the distinctiveness across cases it is difficult to make a blanket assessment about the ultimate impact of participatory budgeting as practiced in the United States in the mold of the 49th Ward. It is clear that context matters quite a bit, particularly in terms of the democratic subject at the center of the process. In New York City the more explicit emphasis on inclusion and participation of the disenfranchised combined with a broad coalition that includes a vast array of social justice organizations and researchers has lent the process a critical and self-reflexive character.[27] It is constantly referenced by New York City activists in immigrant rights and the rights of the formerly incarcerated as a positive example of how to widen citizenship.[28] The Urban Justice Center produces a yearly report that is consistently critical of the limits of the process.[29] Despite this variation the overall process has been by any measure inclusive of the underprivileged, especially when compared to traditional modes of political participation or volunteerism.[30]

Chicago's process in contrast has been less inclusive, tending to privilege the participation of homeowners and college-educated whites.[31]

A 2013 survey of participants in neighborhood assemblies and among community representatives found that Latino participants were severely underrepresented, while African American participants were still underrepresented.[32] Moreover social justice organizations have been largely absent in the overall Chicago process. In one ward researchers report that groups "representing the interests of low-income renters" have been largely absent from the process. Though they "were invited to join," they "were not made to feel welcome" and tried to "disassociate themselves" from participatory budgeting."[33] The same researchers note that "despite the large presence of community groups in Chicago, only a fraction of them were enrolled in the PB process."[34] Vallejo's case sits somewhere between the two other cases—it is slightly less community driven than New York's but more demographically diverse.

The question that remains for us is whether these limited processes have the potential to become more encompassing in their decision making and power of self-regulation. It is clear that the model now in circulation with the imprimatur of success in Chicago and then New York is one that largely excludes administrative reforms and is removed from political-institutional projects; further, a move toward controlling larger sources of funding or having a say over other parts of government machinery does not seem forthcoming. In nearly all of the cities, as in the 49th Ward, frustration is reported in working with city agencies. Conflicts around technical criteria for projects, for example, have often been a source of frustration for participants. In the case of New York technical criteria have been described as "opaque."[35] In some cases conflicts, some muted, some less so, have occurred between established community organizations and new participants. And in most cases there have been disjunctures of the kind we report for the 49th Ward—participants have expected a kind of decision making that is more wide ranging and impactful than the process actually provides for. These manifest in many ways, for example the concern reported in New York that because "PB lacks legal protection" it leaves "unfinished projects vulnerable if a new councilmember leaves office."[36]

In contrast to the Spanish trajectory, where Córdoba's participatory budget helped animate a vision of participation as insurgent and transformative, the trajectory in the United States has largely emphasized collaboration and civic-mindedness. But there are exceptions. One of the most interesting PB processes of the period decided over an *imaginary* budget in Tonawanda, a small town in upstate New York that has the woeful distinction of being one of the most polluted towns in the United States.[37] There, after a long activist campaign, the federal government announced it would fine one of the town's worst polluters, a coke plant, for gross violations of pollution regulations. After the announcement but before the setting of the fine, local activists who drew inspiration from existing U.S. processes ran a PB process in town asking residents how they wanted to use the disbursement.[38] "What would you do with 200 Million Dollars?" posters in town announced, inviting residents to join the budgeting process and alluding to the amount activists *hoped* the actual fine would be. Some six hundred residents participated in the process—more than regularly participate in town hall meetings, activists are quick to point out.[39]

Over the next weeks participants generated dozens of ideas and eventually voted on them, ranking as their first choice a pollution prevention program.[40] Activists then wrote a memo to the judge in charge of determining the fine, asking him to honor community wishes.[41] Although the judge imposed a fine that was only a fraction of the hoped-for $200 million, the final ruling was a victory for activists in that it required that the "defendant fund one or more of the proposed evaluative projects recommended by the community."[42] Emboldened, local environmental activists have imagined other potential processes; one will attempt to decide on the fate of reclaimed land from a retired coal plant and find ways to employ displaced workers, while another will democratize energy production through the participatory process. A local activist noted, "PB is a great tool for us; it's a component of environmental justice that allows us to move." But, she continued, "we're not fighting to change the budget, we're fighting to change the system."

CHAPTER SIX

The Utopian Undercurrent
of Participation

There is no lack of worrying about the state of democracy in the world today, in which democracy's symbolic victory over any other alternative sits paradoxically alongside two facts: the increasing rule of economic interests over all other concerns, and widespread disaffection with democratic institutions. More and more, democracy appears to be spreading while its meaning seems to be ever more modest. There are more ways than ever to participate democratically today, but the range of decisions within the reach of the demos seems narrower than ever. "We are all democrats now," writes Wendy Brown, but as her essay also poignantly asks, "what is left of democracy?"[1]

The two cases of participatory budgeting in Córdoba and in Chicago's 49th Ward were small instances in much bigger contexts. Each mobilized relatively small pools of participants to decide over circumspect budgetary set-asides. The process in Córdoba came undone under fire from organized civil society groups, while Chicago's process never managed to mobilize very diverse participants. Neither case propelled very significant changes in community mobilization or existing patterns of governmental routines. Nonetheless they served as powerful demonstrations that participatory budgeting could "work" in their respective contexts—Córdoba serving as an important model for Spain and Europe, and the 49th Ward becoming one of the templates emulated throughout North America.

Efforts like these are emblematic of the contemporary moment of participation and are consistent with how we have come to understand democratic innovations. The objective of the new spirit of government, as we have discussed, is primarily to connect government with citizens. Those who promote democratic innovations today believe these projects effectively "fight apathy" and want to place citizens at the center of governance. Democratic innovations rely heavily on the concept of deliberation, draw on participation from ordinary people, and value inclusion for its own sake. At its core participatory budgeting as instantiated in both sites was a process that brings more voices to the table and allows citizens to debate the common good. Participatory budgeting, like other democratic innovations today, is understood as a compelling way to gather governmental input, build trust in government, and create communities of engaged citizens. More sanguine promoters hold the view that participation, properly instituted, can help solve all kinds of modern-day problems of governance and politics.[2]

Seldom addressed by mainstream promoters of participation though is the question of subjecting real societal and state power to the decision making emerging out of that participation. There is little talk today of publics mobilized by, say, "deliberative circles," becoming what Nancy Fraser distinguishes as *empowered* publics or, in those kinds of debates, the kind of real-utopian empowered participatory governance Archon Fung and Erik Olin Wright advocate.[3] As a result of this lack many critics have come to argue that contemporary configurations of participation constitute nothing more than a new form of management of conduct characteristic of the neoliberal era—at best a fantasy, or in Andrew Thompson's evocative phrase, a pantomime of real democracy.[4] The missing element for critics, that of popular sovereignty, is indeed largely not present in the cases in this book or in today's democratic innovations. It would be difficult to say that the two cases we discuss here subject significant forms of state or societal power to the participatory forums they assembled. The budgets they decided over were small fractions of much larger budgets and remained bound by broader technocratic mandates. And it would be difficult to claim they addressed or exerted any influence over the most salient issues facing residents in either place, be it unemployment, police violence, or the lack of affordable housing.

But that is not the end of the story. Contemporary participation, as in the cases in this book, *can* include a quite radical element, which is the ideal of inclusive discussion of common circumstances, and which actually stands in sharp contrast to neoliberal ideals of atomized consumer-citizens. This formation of a self-questioning demos evinces the idea of sovereignty, which makes the whole arrangement potentially quite unstable. To put it another way, we think that critics underappreciate how contemporary participatory institutions such as those described here are not necessarily limited by their stated goals and procedures. They inadvertently invite questions they do not answer and as such are fundamentally ambiguous. In practice, as in the cases in this book, they can be tension filled, caught between goals of good governance and forms of participation that can outrun them. Whether participatory arrangements actually provide such openings for more expansive forms of participation, and what that might mean, or remain mired in a thicket of procedures, expert closure, and pantomime, is a larger question. In this concluding chapter we probe our cases for clues to an answer.

The Ambiguities of Deliberation without Rule

While we share the concerns of critics, our approach has also been fundamentally empirical: by tracing the movement and implementation of one particular instrument across sites, we have sought to reflect on what we can learn about the potentials and limits of participation today. Much like the story of Porto Alegre's PB (Chapter 3), the development of participatory budgeting elsewhere was shaped as much by conflicts and controversies as by conscious efforts to enroll allies in projects as they grew. And like Porto Alegre these controversies tended to be less present in how-to guides or in many subsequent accounts. As we noted, during the early years of the participatory processes in Chicago and Córdoba, there were some obvious manifestations of unstated rules about the limits of the process as they provoked controversies. We described these in some detail, not in the interest of exposing some "secret history" of participation nor to take away from the real accomplishments of participants and implementers. Rather these controversies represent "limit situations" and hint at paths not taken. These key moments functioned as sites of resistance and also pushed the reformulation of political horizons.

Underlying struggles for power and authority, between and among participants and city officials, were in effect negotiations over profound questions about who represents certain communities and who determines the legitimacy of citizen demands. Both Chicago and Córdoba demonstrated these complex dynamics between citizens and the administrative machineries of local governments, and revealed an otherwise hidden line of separation between the rule of experts and collective citizen knowledge. PB opened up a new space of autonomy for citizens to empower themselves, often in opposition to local administrations. It provided citizens, many of whom were accustomed to their marginal role in public service, direct contact with their local government officials. This contact, and the resulting tensions and debates, implicitly and explicitly challenged the legitimacy of the status quo. These dynamics turned PB's implementation process into a discussion about who speaks for the community, about morality and democracy, and about the value of different types of knowledge, positioning the "vague, selfish, and contingent" citizen against the "objective and accurate" expert.

Attention to these conflicts reframes the criticism of political theorists like Mouffe, Zizek, Dean, Brown, Rancière, and others who worry about the displacement of fundamental questions in contemporary democratic institutions. Looked at closely, the Chicago and Córdoba PB experiments did not so clearly fit with this characterization. Residents frequently resisted the logic and limits of the process, claiming their own conceptions of association, freedom, and sovereignty. Participants asserted that they, as citizens, were entitled to question expertise, to demand specified projects for their communities, to be "self-interested," and to challenge the claims of community leaders. Propitiously it was actually when participation seemed to break down in moments of ambiguity and indecision that the inquisitive dialogue most prized by democratic theorists emerged.

In Chicago and Córdoba participants engaged in inquisitive and reflexive conversations, and focused on collective problems. Their communication embodied values presented in this new age of participation: the importance of communicative rationality, unmediated voice, and the political turn toward the common. But the conversations also demonstrated what Lisa Wedeen would refer to as an "as-if" quality.[5] In both Chicago and Córdoba participants often assumed that participatory institutions were more far-reaching than they actually were. Discussions sometimes took place *as if* citizens really ran city government, *as if* they really had power over technical rules, and *as if* they really could control (and not just discuss) the outcomes of decisions that impacted them, including the shape and format of participation itself. Indeed conversations took place that reached in the direction of popular sovereignty.

Their rhetoric evidences what Castoriadis called the capacity of groups to imagine alternative futures and new norms of self-regulation. For Castoriadis the creative imagination is universal and involves a combination of individual and social processes. The individual's ability to imagine new worlds holds the potential for citizens to enter public life and transcend existing patterns of thought and behavior. Yet according to Castoriadis, the social world we inherit and the norms that guide social action form imagination in the first place and limit the potential of imagination to institute new worlds. He calls this creative and collective ability the "social instituting imaginary," highlighting that political activity involves both imagining new worlds and instituting them, or bringing them to life.[6]

Democratic innovations can, in our reading, push the imagination of citizens beyond the logic of representation. The principles of coordination of new participatory instruments can open these vistas: there is no longer a need to justify deliberation against expert knowledge; it is not necessary to hide the value of citizens' voices nor their concern for the common good. This participatory age is also built from a more radical feature of democracy, the participation of all in political decisions. Participants in these spaces today speak from these baseline assumptions. Such rhetoric served the residents of Chicago and Córdoba to challenge the symbolic holders of civil authority and administrative knowledge.

Faced with the threat of depoliticization, Chicago and Córdoba citizens appealed to the worldly sense of democracy, whose object is not the struggle between antagonistic subjects or the goal of achieving predetermined ends, but the advent of equality and the chance to question rules within this political context. For Rancière that is the field in which we can speak today of emancipation, not to found a counterpower "susceptible of governing a future society" but "to effect the demonstration of capacity, which is also a demonstration of community. Self-emancipation is not secession, but self-affirmation as a joint-sharer in a common world, appearances to the contrary notwithstanding, assuming that you can play the same game as the adversary."[7] There is nothing more radical politically than to resignify the public space as a space of equals.

The difficulties of new participatory processes have been widely mentioned in previous chapters. If it is true that the defense of this space of equals urges citizens to resist and to think of alternatives, then the role of governments in generating misunderstandings about its scope is no less true. Imagined worlds of popular sovereignty have collided with existing institutions, habits, and the established powers. The latter would limit the space of equals to the exchange of views and keep authority in a black box; thus the critical space from which citizens might test mechanisms and be empowered to construct alternatives is hidden and diffuse. In Chicago and Córdoba, however, participants went beyond questioning authority and insisted on a more transparent and direct relationship. The social imagination, as Castoriadis said, allows us to advance futures and realities.

In the remainder of this chapter we follow this line of thinking to its logical conclusion and explore participation's radical imaginary. We reach into the past to recover a model of participation that is centered on the idea of popular sovereignty, which is both democratic and endowed with power. We then briefly return to the pitfalls of democracy without sovereignty before discussing how even limited forms of participation may provide fodder for realizing imagined futures.

Sovereign Participation

Porto Alegre's original undertaking in participatory budgeting was quite a radical experiment in participatory democracy. Before the experiment became a best practice, it was part of a renewed transformative project, a tool to resolve the endemic problems of the leftists in power. In addition to open meetings where citizens decided on priorities, Porto Alegre's PB relied on a much less visible but crucially important institutional architecture. This structure created the conditions for decisions to be meaningful by linking them to the centers of governmental decision making. The state instituted several real democratic reforms, which among others included mandates to subordinate the local bureaucracy to citizen demands and to protect the "chain of popular sovereignty" from outside influence by creating a cabinet-level special department. The open meetings combined with these reforms allowed PB participation to operate as an effective popular control mechanism of the local state.

This combination has been why participatory budgeting, in this version, has been so generative for the "real utopias" project as developed by Fung and Wright.[8] It connected specifically with their discussion of *empowered* participatory governance. The empowered participatory governance proposal is an institutional design for deliberative decision making and pragmatic problem solving among participants over a specific common good. In principle it is applicable to a wide range of situations, and it centers on reforms that devolve decision making to local units supported, but not directed, by a central body. In turn these units are genuinely empowered to enact their own decisions. This model aims to foster redistributive and efficient decision making that is deliberative and democratic, and superior to command-and-control structures on a number of counts.

We describe these two sides of participatory budgeting—participation and administration reform—as the communicative and the sovereignty dimensions of PB. We use the term *communicative dimension* to describe the open structure of transparent meetings to deliberate on projects and priorities. We chose this term because the meetings are based on procedures that regulate the conditions of communication, thus democratizing the nature of demand making in civil society and opening the forum to the plurality of opinions in the city. The *sovereignty dimension* refers to the connection of those meetings to the centers of decision making within the administration.[9]

From the point of view of the community activists who first conceived of participatory budgeting, analytically separating it into two dimensions—communication and sovereignty—would have been illogical. Nonetheless for analytic purposes and with the benefit of hindsight, it is worth returning to those sets of questions. The case of the city of Porto Alegre itself is especially instructive, where after defeating the Workers' Party in late 2004, a politically conservative coalition took power. This coalition maintained superficial features of PB while returning the actual functioning of the administration to more traditional modes of patronage and privileging of local elites. Similarly, research on the numerous participatory forums established by the national Workers' Party administration in Brazil (2003–present) has shown that a semblance of radical democracy can coexist with quite conservative policies.[10]

The Communicative Dimension of Participatory Budgeting

Democratic deliberation is today the best-known feature of participatory budgeting. In Brazil, PB processes were designed to match the municipal budgeting cycle; accordingly, meetings were organized around a schedule of government-sponsored sessions that began early in the year, around March or April, and ended in November. All processes began with assemblies, or open meetings, throughout the town or city and ended when participants selected projects to include in the yearly budget. Most of the democratic discussion and deliberation took place in the assemblies. At the outset these served to inform participants about the procedures and available resources; later, participants proposed and debated particular projects, and representatives were chosen. The last assemblies were devoted to making the final decisions on the budget. Typically, PB processes drew large numbers of participants—in some cases in Brazil as much as 10 percent of the total population of a town attended a meeting.

Much of the scholarship on Porto Alegre and on Brazil refers to PB meetings as a public sphere. Indeed many scholars perceive self-rule in PB as a deliberative process,[11] closer to Habermas's theory than accounts of direct democracy or theories of radical democracy.[12] In contrast to decisions, deliberative theory relies on opinion. The general will should be built from citizens' opinions. But there are significant differences between the deliberative framework and the PB process. For the former, political self-rule takes place in two stages: first there is an informal discussion outside institutions (in the "lifeworld"), and then follows a formalization of this debate with public input that seeks to influence institutional actions. Scholars generally understand that social movements form the key link between the two stages because they have the power to amplify demands in the public space. Porto Alegre's participatory budget changed this scheme within a participatory framework. What for Habermas and others was a natural sequence of informal discussions that began in the lifeworld and was then carried forward by social movements to the political system gave way in Porto Alegre to formal discussions bounded by procedures and a direct influence on policy.

The participatory budget proposal brought the thinking behind the deliberative turn into a participatory institutional framework. The principal difference between PB and deliberative democratic theory has to do with the link between public discussion and government. In a purely deliberative sense, citizens' influence on government is highly contingent on their ability to frame a problem and mobilize allies, and there is a wide separation between rulers and the ruled. Scholars used to talk about an informal sovereignty dimension.[13] This sequence gives rise to many questions, for example how can informal spaces guarantee an equal treatment for citizens' opinions? Participatory budgeting, on the contrary, aims to rationally translate bottom-up demands and to structure the nature of those communications according to procedures. Within the participatory budgeting model the administration organizes public spaces dominated by deliberative frameworks.

Deliberative proposals generally underestimate the value of establishing transparent procedures in the formation of opinion. One of the major criticisms of deliberative theory is precisely this: in the informal sphere not everyone participates and gives an opinion with the same intensity. The capacity then for citizens to be heard and to imagine themselves a part of the political space is not distributed proportionally.[14] When citizens see their efforts to express their opinion as futile, democracy fails—the link that justifies democracy and its worldly sense is broken. For many contemporary scholars political disaffection lies in that broken link.[15] By structuring the space of opinion through procedures, democratic innovation, in particular PB, formally matches that effort. This does not solve gender or other imbalances among participants, or self-selection when citizens participate, but it does allow everyone to imagine a transparent procedure for participation.[16]

The opinion structured by procedures does entail democratic risks. Perhaps the most important is the risk of closing the spaces of dissent. Proceedings are time delimited, for example, opening the possibility for procedural control over what is deemed feasible and what is not. That is why deliberative theory has always strongly defended the informal nature of public opinion,[17] in which opinion is buffered against potential uniformity and processes of domination. The problem here, however, is a weakening of the imaginary link between citizens and their rulers, between opinion and will. With this disconnection the liberal spirit has often opposed freedom of speech and equal opportunity.[18] Indeed the freedom to speak is disconnected from sovereignty, which requires the same procedures for all.

Deliberative theory offers us a counterfactual standard against which we can test the communicative dimension of PB as a process of democratization and against its democratic risks. For deliberative scholars the formation of political will starts in a debate between individuals in the public space, in the context of shared understandings. These debates take place under specific conditions: inclusion (nobody can be excluded from participation in a discussion that interests them); freedom from coercion (anyone can take part in the argument and counterargument freely without being subject to domination by others); and openness (each participant can start and continue the discussion on any relevant topic, including the procedures regulating the discussion).[19] Moving this critical framework to participatory budgeting and democratic innovations gives us several counterfactual standards against which we can judge specific experiences and their procedures:

1. What is the intensity of the participation? Who actually participates? Do features of participatory spaces prevent these processes from being open to all?

2. How inclusive is the deliberation? In addition to being present at assemblies, do all citizens "deliberate"? Are there systematic biases about who speaks and who decides? Is the technical language made accessible to all?

3. How democratic is the deliberation? What is the quality of decisions emanating from the participatory process? Do participants feel free to openly debate or discuss the rules governing discussions?[20]

The scholarship on participatory budgeting in Brazil and other countries has addressed the communicative dimension quite carefully, and research efforts continue to focus on "participant surveys." But self-rule does not subsist only in communication. The second facet of participatory budgeting is the coupling of PB assemblies with administrative structures. We refer to this as the sovereignty dimension.

The Sovereignty Dimension

For Habermas and much of civil society theory, the link between deliberation and public policy occurs through the mediation of political and social organizations.[21] Participatory budgeting, in contrast, sets up an institutionalized link to administration. PB relies on deliberative processes to determine proposals (valued for their reasonableness in noncoercive and egalitarian spaces) and joins these proposals with government actions. The singular process that opened in the Brazilian experience was to do it through real democratic reforms of the state apparatus. As we describe below, this coupling stemmed from more than merely the political will to respond to popular demands: the administration comprehensively reorganized its structures to accommodate the PB process.

These reforms included the creation of a direct and exclusive link between forums and decisions; a set of changes in the bureaucracy so that the administration would be able to process those decisions; and a forum for what political theorists sometimes refer to as "second-order" discussions, the discussions about the general principles that guide more specific discussions. This in our view enabled the deliberative forums on urban infrastructure—as novel as they were in the 1990s—to become an *experiment that restructured social space*. In this new space we can glimpse political self-rule and the utopian ideal of a political project based on participation. To build this new democratic space there were three less visible institutional reforms—because they took place within administration—which we call the (exclusive) conveyor belt, bureaucratic participatory reforms, and the forum of forums.

First, the image of an (exclusive) conveyor belt illustrates a transparent institutional link between popular will and government actions. Each participant had a minimum number of veto points and room for discretionary changes. The "chain of popular sovereignty" was protected from the moment decisions were made to their implementation. This for example included an annual edition of the easily accessed and widely understood "book of projects," which listed when projects were decided, how they were funded, and the timeline of their completion. If any technical changes or amendments appeared along the way, municipal workers notified participants. The administration created a new budget planning office that centralized management accounts and PB, and positioned this administrative body above municipal departments to ensure impartiality in implementation.[22] This new budget planning office, placed above the municipal offices, applied criteria emerging from participatory forums to the allocation of public resources among departments. Instead of reinforcing back-room negotiations within the administration to secure resources, the new system removed politicians from the competition. Every citizen had the chance to reference the "book of projects" to look at and test the entire process.

The conveyor belt served as the exclusive point of contact between government and citizens through administrative reforms. Channels for citizen demands other than the PB process were essentially closed; that is, the general population made contact with the administration almost exclusively through the PB process. Certainly in Porto Alegre it became impossible to access funds, investments, or city projects out-side of the participatory process.

Second, the administration set up complex institutional arrange-ments to prepare its machinery to accept these inputs. For "participa-tion to come to the administration" it was necessary to create new patterns and practices within the administration. In addition to the direct, institutionalized links between participation and government action (which implied centralization), administrative machinery was decentralized.[23] The administration recognized that bureaucrats and offices were accustomed to dealing with different sorts of inputs than those developed at neighborhood assemblies by the city's less privi-leged residents. All municipal departments were thus required to cre-ate the position of "community facilitator." Community facilitators would serve as the "face" of each municipal department in each of the city's districts. They were required to attend PB meetings with the express purpose of helping participants prepare technically viable proj-ects and to be accountable for ongoing projects. In short, these fa-cilitators were responsible for serving as the liaison between the com-munity and technical experts within the departments. All community facilitators attended a weekly forum to keep participatory processes coherent. As much as possible, "technical expertise was to be made subordinate to the popular mandate, and not the other way around," as one facilitator described in an interview.[24]

Third, a higher tier of participatory structures served an important "forum of forums" function, called the Municipal Council of the Budget. This council brought together representatives from various stages in the process. Its purpose was to debate and legitimate the process as a whole. The council members addressed unexpected events beyond PB's defined parameters; they deliberated and decided on the rules of the process; they set broad investment priorities according to abstract social justice criteria; and they acted as intermediaries between the municipal government and local participants. This forum of forums provided participants with the ability to self-regulate the process and engage an often heated debate about general principles that would ultimately shape administrative public policies.

The combination of communicative and sovereignty dimensions led to significant consequences. First, through the Council of the Budget participants were able to change the social justice criteria and the rules of the process. They were also able to influence how much the administration dedicated municipal resources to the process. They were, in other words, able to change the dynamic of their participation in its relationship to the government. The process provided a clear counterfactual against which participants and observers could evaluate (and test) the exercise of power, hindering a devolution into charismatic authority. But perhaps more dramatically it allowed the administration to carry out a pro-poor policy under a new legitimated political framework based on social justice criteria. Applying these criteria, the administration gave priority to proposals arising from the PB process and distributed the budget among different municipal areas while setting up the management of institutional policies. PB thus offered a unique way to articulate participation and sovereignty within modern political arrangements. For former Porto Alegre mayor Raul Pont, PB was an alternative to the historic dilemma faced by representative democracy; that is, how to accommodate power with participation and social justice.[25] In contrast to an earlier Latin American tradition on the left, PB placed the political debate about emancipation and participation within representative institutions.

Acknowledging the sovereignty dimension thus invites us to not only consider deliberative intensity and quality but also to examine the intensity with which participants can qualify and sort their preferences. Looking at the sovereignty dimension also allows us to think about the intensity of the connection between participation and the exercise of authority. The sovereignty dimension has, for us, four distinct but interrelated criteria against which to judge other experiments:

1. The primacy of the participatory forums. If the participatory forums are not the exclusive point of contact between government and citizen, how important of a point of contact are they? Are there other ways of accessing government resources, and how important are those?

2. The scope and importance of administrative issues that are subjected to participation. How much of the local budget is subjected to participation, and how important is that budget to social justice efforts?

3. The degree of actual participatory power over the budget. Are there institutionalized, direct, and transparent links between participation and government action? What if any administrative reforms are undertaken to prepare the state apparatus to receive participatory inputs? What discretion do elected officials, technical staff, and bureaucrats have over the decisions once they are made?

4. Participation's self-regulating, or constitutional aspect. To what extent are participants able to determine the rules of participation; to debate and determine social justice criteria that will order the process; to determine the reach of participatory influence over government affairs?

Global Expansion of Participation: Pitfalls

If we were to take our sets of questions about communication and sovereignty to today's "how-to" manuals and to currently circulating blueprints for participatory budgeting, the result would be to show that processes seldom include anything but the communicative dimension. Toolkits and blueprints generally only include the first dimension, having little to say about the second, which is understood to depend entirely on local implementation. The real democratic reforms and connectors between communication and state actions are frequently "black-boxed." This does not mean, however, that the sovereignty dimension is necessarily missing in every experiment, but only that it is largely contingent on the will of local representatives. Toolkits for global implementation often emphasize the yearly cycle of meetings, rules for open and transparent assemblies, and how to carry out voting procedures on proposals. They say little about how reforms enable those proposals' compatibility with administrative logics. These toolkits fail to describe mechanisms that would allow participants to define the terms of participation or how to make those the primary interfaces.

Indeed, looking then at the many global cases of PB, we find a commonality around the set of meetings to discuss investments, but these are embedded within diverse national and political contexts that dictate the overall priority and purpose of the participatory budget. Normally the focus is on citizen apathy rather than social justice or political transformation. Thus local projects are rarely successful at implementing sovereignty reforms. As we have already expressed, we worry that PB becomes a participatory experience that leaves citizens thinking collectively about trivial issues from the standpoint of the administration of power, as has so often been the case with traditional participatory devices.[26] And as some recent research has shown, this is happening in all kinds of participatory experiences.[27] From this context the deep skepticism of citizens about their ability to influence policy making is justified, because the prevailing division of powers between public authorities and citizens is far from being challenged.[28]

From the point of view of an emancipatory project, the reduction of PB to the communicative dimension with limited elements of sovereignty poses at least three fundamental problems. First, as we have suggested throughout, participation can become disconnected from the decisions that matter most to communities.[29] Practitioners often attempt to implement participatory budgeting through the path of least resistance. Thus, these processes become connected to small, discretionary budgets. This can lead to community organizing around issues outside social justice frameworks or, worse, to PB projects being dictated by administrative possibilities rather than more autonomous conversations about community and individual needs.[30] A second problem is that participants might come to understand participation as a technical solution rather than as a political tactic of emancipation. It happens when citizens are unable to debate second-order issues. A third concern is that a high degree of discretion over participation's outcomes remains in the hands of others. In this situation politicians can hijack the process to legitimize charismatic authority or demobilize communities that have invested time and energy into processes. Such corrupted processes can result in a community's understanding of the participatory project as a sham. Along these lines some studies on PB experiences have indeed shown their weak impact on the dynamics of municipalities, even when practitioners devised the experiences with an emancipatory rhetoric in mind.[31]

Faced with the limits of PB's global implementations, Graham Smith invites us to think about participatory budgeting in relationship to past practices rather than against alleged unfulfilled promises.[32] Participatory budgeting can certainly improve on previous participatory practices by expanding the political subject, establishing and guiding deliberative procedures, and at the very least allowing citizens to take a position on budget reforms. Yves Sintomer, in his global research on PB, points out that this is one of the few common denominators that we find among the experiments around the world.[33] We have argued elsewhere that the democratization of civil society is important,[34] but it is not inherent to participatory projects, as studies have sometimes revealed disappointing outcomes.[35] Recent research on PB for example has analyzed its impact on civil society in Brazil,[36] China,[37] Africa,[38] and Europe[39]—the latter with mixed results.[40] While the democratization of civil society does have important implications, we would hazard the guess that it is often contingent on whether participation is truly empowered over issues of concern; in other words, whether it is sovereign.

Toward a Critical Ethic of Translation: Breaking with the Technocratic Mold

Looking at the story of participatory budgeting globally does not yield a simple "neoliberalization of participation" story as much as one of institutional delinking as a precondition for PB's travel in the neoliberal era. In spite of invocations of social justice by some of its implementers, over time participatory budgeting has become effectively decoupled from progressive institutional projects and from the idea of administrative reform.

In analytic terms this makes PB close to what sociologists of science call a *mutable mobile*, referring to "objects that have to adapt and change shape if they are to survive" while maintaining a surface similarity. John Law and Annemarie Mol give the example of the diffusion of the bush pump in Sub-Saharan Africa, which serves as a useful image here.[41] These pumps were very widely adopted, and taken at one point as evidence of a kind of diffusion of cultural modernization; on closer inspection it was only surface features of the pump that remained constant—its handle and its outward appearance.

Subterranean features (plumbing and pipes); who used the pump; and what defined a successful pump were quite different from village to village.

In this way participatory budgeting is no different from many other traveling blueprints: some parts of the idea travel at the expense of others, and important dynamics need to be understood in the process of promoting the idea in this global moment, as well as its instantiation in any particular context. Sergio Montero's excellent research on the travel of bus rapid transit technologies from Brazil to Colombia and then to the world makes a similar point.[42] Other investigations might be undertaken on the trajectories of the solidarity economy, citizen juries, users' councils, microcredit schemes, gender budgeting, urban cooperatives, and fair trade among many other traveling best practices. Jamie Peck and Nik Theodore's recent fifteen-country opus on the travel of participatory budgeting and conditional cash transfer confirms the general outlines of the argument we have made here.[43]

But the story also tells of the significant power of those doing the translation between places: the mediators, experts, PowerPoint presentations, how-to manuals, and academic and newspaper articles that pass the idea along as they promote it. Certainly those who implement and translate democratic innovations like participatory budgeting may encounter strong pressure from administrators or philanthropic funders for a participatory process to be treated as an end in itself. It is our understanding though that experts may have more room for maneuvering than they generally imagine themselves to have. The expert presentation of PB as value-neutral may feel necessary to introduce it in certain contexts, and this can narrow the grounds for reopening the discussion to speak for sovereignty reforms. Indeed the line drawn between expertise and advocacy may make it difficult for technical experts to advocate on behalf of more expansive moves. Similarly, although allowing narrow, technocratic measures for what constitutes "success"—such as numbers of participants in a meeting, consumerlike perceptions of satisfaction, or even instilling so-called democratic values—may seem like a necessary concession at first, much evidence suggests that such measures have a way of eventually driving projects. One of the changes with the global travel of PB has been the creation of *dedicated* PB networks (in which both authors have participated), which have tended over time to become dissociated from other discussions of participatory democracy or from discussions about cities and social justice. Relatedly, instead of being part of a broader political project, PB has become a platform in itself. This narrowing has come at a significant cost, closing off space for the articulation of other concerns, and connecting institutional survival to the application of participatory budgeting blueprints. It might just be that for particular issues such as police violence or global trade agreements, non-budgeting-related participatory reforms might have much more valence. As a fundamental corollary we feel it is important for implementers to begin participatory projects with actual community needs and desires in mind, and not just develop projects around feasible budgets and goals as if participation was good in itself or drawing people to meetings was in itself a desirable goal.

Archon Fung has soberly warned that even though "many participatory democrats hope that participatory governance reforms will also advance social justice," this is not merely a technical problem or "a problem of institutional design." The challenge is instead "political. In most contexts, the organizations and leaders who possess the resources and authority to create significant participatory governance initiatives simply lack the motivation to advance social justice through those projects."[44] We would urge implementers to also think politically in this way, connecting with other movements that are in different ways working toward sovereignty and democratic control. The range of potential allies here is wide, and it is important to think creatively about how to enroll them.

In the case of the United States for example, living-wage activists, anti-police-violence campaigns, and anti-big-box retail organizers may not seem like immediate allies from the narrow point of view of shared interest in infrastructure investments, but all of these groups are working on empowering state reforms. Similarly PB campaigns should not lose sight of controlling meaningful budgets, even if they must start with imaginary versions. Without a connection between communication and sovereignty, the most sensible path for PB is its being implemented through the path of least resistance; that is, through budgets of less importance to bureaucrats and powerful interests. In Europe and North America, for example, PB processes have addressed small portions of discretionary funds of budgets, usually urban infrastructure. These processes do not undertake larger portions directed at economic development, for example. In many cases it appears too complicated to start with those; yet it is important not to forget them.

But the global travel story also yields a complex picture with potential openings. Unlike the story of some other documented traveling blueprints, this one is not so clearly attached to particular bodies of expertise or professional certification or exclusively to powerful international agencies. Loose ideas about "participation" and even about participatory budgeting are more like objects that travel in "ideoscapes," those constant flows of "ideas, terms and images, including 'freedom,' 'welfare,' 'rights,' 'sovereignty.'" The sources of these ideas are manifold; their coherence is loose; and multiple local interpretations are always possible.[45]

Among the dozen or so experiences in the United States for example, all more or less modeled on the Chicago template, there is significant variation in the interpretation of participation's political potential. New York City's experience (2011–present), led by social justice organizations and organized around "inclusion" and "empowerment," has been an inclusive and quite open process. In sharp contrast to Chicago's process, here the process was driven by a community organization with a mission to empower underprivileged residents of New York City. "We're striving in PB for participation that represents the true diversity in which people live, and making special efforts to engage the populations that are often left out or disconnected, and yet have so much at stake."[46] Others, like Chicago's 49th Ward, have continued to be less inclusive, tending to privilege the participation of homeowners and college-educated whites, while Latino and black participants are underrepresented.[47] And the relationship to community organizations is highly variable across the United States. In New York, as we have seen, social justice organizations constitute the backbone of the process, while in Chicago the process is filled with more "civic-minded" organizations, largely "neighborhood associations, block clubs, CDCs, arts groups, chambers of commerce, and park advisory councils." The same researchers note that "despite the large presence of community groups in Chicago, only a fraction of them were enrolled in the PB process";[48] some researchers have described it as a "top-down mobilization" strategy closely linked to the alderman's apparatus.

Particularly because the proponents of participatory budgeting can be so different, it is possible at any one site for experts and implementers to run up against quite divergent local interpretations of what PB can be. There are profound contradictions and ambiguities in the travel of participatory budgeting, and it is in exploiting those that we see some openings for more progressive interventions. Returning to these ambiguous aspects can occasion productive tensions and the potential to repoliticize participation. Each of these ambiguities can provide the space for claims making by participants and others to resist "expert closure" and push the boundaries of participation toward meaningful decision making over the conditions that affect their own lives.[49]

Beyond Communication, beyond Budgets: Participation as Emancipation

The architecture of modern liberal political institutions revolves around the precautionary principle. The Madisonian republic did not just propose to neutralize the innate selfishness of people, in particular politicians; it was founded on their mistrust of one another. This distrust led to the creation of technical institutions with a sovereign capacity to decide on issues affecting citizens.[50] Such institutions are in principle prized for their impartiality, which lends them legitimacy as being able to rise above particular interests.[51] Alongside their development, a major professional role emerged, that of a new elite able to technically handle social problems and therefore manage public affairs without ideological and political bias. In the early 1980s Christopher Lasch called this "the revolution of the elites."[52] Politics as a professional matter is, so to speak, the counter-imagination of participatory projects.

On the other hand, the present democratization process of our participatory age is paradoxical. In contrast to the protests in Paris and Berkeley in the 1960s, the current participatory wave since the early 2000s is governmentally driven. In many cities of the Global North democratic innovations such as participatory budgets do not come from and have never been used by social movements in the cities in which they are eventually adopted. Participation today is no longer only a utopian desire from the grass roots; it is now part of the way power works. It is, as we have described it, democratization from above.

Yet recent movements in Europe for example have led not to new social movements but rather to new political platforms such as Podemos or Syrizia, which are willing to manage the public from another perspective. Political stirrings in North America are similar. And this changes the focus yet again. These projects do not compete in the public space to influence political outcomes or policies; instead they would change the process of making politics altogether. In these new utopias the spatial configuration of power is horizontal, a society of equals that calls into question all hierarchies.[53]

It is clear that repoliticization of public affairs cannot be done solely through the communicative dimension. No amount of "deliberative circles" or empty exercises in fostering conversation for its own sake will achieve it. These new political utopias are not about creating spaces of discussion but about linking those discussions to sovereign decision making. Habermas believed that communication was a solution to Weber's diagnosis of the inevitability of instrumental domination in complex societies. As much as Weber thought of the omnivorous power of the bureaucracy, Habermas argued that communication would prevent a total domination by instrumental rationality. From our point of view, imagining these horizontal political spaces must be linked to the administration and distribution of power, because what is at stake is not only an exchange of opinions but a process of *decision making in public affairs and the practical consequences.*

For this to be realized, participation must lead to taking stances whose consequences can be assessed by the participants. The participants of Córdoba understood this well when they raised the need for the citizens' "right to be wrong," or to make decisions that were less desirable from a technocratic point of view—as did participants in Chicago when they prepared PowerPoint presentations to defend their ideas about bike paths.

The challenge of the contemporary political crisis that we are living through is to imagine a democracy of equals as a fully realized institutional project. It is not, for us, about the struggle for power within given institutions but about a struggle to transform the very relationship between society and its institutions.[54] It is about imagining and instantiating institutions that derive their legitimacy not from impartiality and professionalism, as in Madison's view, but from their ability to reflect the demos and rootedness in it. The battle for democracy today lies not only in thinking of better-functioning institutions or in making them more inclusive or further reaching. The battle is much more radical, and the stakes are higher, having to do with the advent of the democratic regime whereby all can be part of the political community, making decisions over matters of import.

In and of themselves, contemporary participatory instruments, like those in this book, only bring us part of the way. Much as we have argued for Chicago and Córdoba, Celina Su, reflecting on New York's case, notes that participatory budgeting has been impressive in beginning to reframe who is counted as part of the community, "working against a deficit model of formerly incarcerated youth as troublemakers or undocumented immigrants as a drain on the welfare state" and creating a radically broader sense of the demos. Yet, she writes, "there remain challenges in shifting dynamics of power between political stakeholders and governmental agencies, with contestations over who represents the public here, and what sorts of knowledge should be valued in what ways, and how equity ought to be best defined and achieved."[55]

The problem in our view is ultimately not a lack of instruments, nor their operational framework, but the very real resistance to open up political spaces horizontally. Successful instruments clearly exist, but the difficulty lies in extending their reach over decisions that are ultimately more meaningful to the communities in question. To extend the logic of participatory budgeting, say to exert power over policing or zoning, and to indeed transform the relationship between communities and the very process of making those policies will involve power struggles of an entirely greater magnitude than currently experienced. There are nonetheless examples of specific transformations that point us that way, using contemporary participatory instruments and radicalizing them in the direction of popular sovereignty. In the already mentioned case of the newly elected officials in Madrid, the city has announced it will implement participatory budgeting alongside an initiative that will allow citizens to propose rules, laws, and specific policies, with the aim of entirely supplanting politicians and representative democracy. In Berlin, through a referendum, Berliners were able to get the government to remunicipalize water management inspired by Bolivian experiments in community control of public resources.[56]

Participation as emancipation means for us a radical recovery of public grounds—not a specific public order but a public process to handle public issues. This does not imply that everyone should constantly be participating, or that professionals or experts should disappear; it does mean that everyone, including lay citizens, is aware that they can participate at any time in a transparent and deliberative process as part of an empowered community of equals over issues of common concern. This for us would include participation in second-order issues as well as the range of issues that affect the conditions of individual and collective life. It certainly includes collectively determining the conditions of the participation itself and very much implies participation in both local and translocal issues (some of the crucial issues of our time, such as climate change or the global regulation of international capital, will not be solved by local forums). The architecture of such a collective order has been barely glimpsed, but we believe it includes combinations of different sorts of participatory formats, including complex articulations between local and translocal forums. Important insights into what this might look like have been variously developed in the specific proposals of Empowered Participatory Governance, the "Next System Project," and some of the thinking emerging out of the World Social Forums, among others. As all of these proposals suggest, these participatory forums would be vested with vast regulatory powers, including power over private enterprise.

Today's democratic innovations are in the end profoundly paradoxical. They democratize but their impulse does not emerge from below. They assemble communities to discuss matters of common concern, but they do not endow them with the decision making to impact those decisions. They raise questions that cannot be answered within their own parameters. Their democratic quality is highly dependent on social movements, associational groupings, and political parties, but they do not recognize those groups as interlocutors.

Sometimes they fail to survive, as in Córdoba, but their failure ignites a more radical imagination that will live on in other institutional projects, as in Spain. And sometimes they succeed in drawing participants and in being repeated in subsequent yearly cycles, yet at the cost of a more expansive understanding of democracy. But even in low-profile processes decoupled from political projects or broader reforms, the logic of participation anchored in direct decision making can collide with institutional structures set up for something else. The question for activists, implementers, and engaged scholars alike is whether we can make the most of those collisions and the critical energies they summon in order to expand the realm of the possible.

Notes

Chapter One: The Participation Age

1. "Forum Mondial de la Démocratie."

2. "The United States releases its Second Open Government National Action Plan."

3. "The Open Government Partnership Second Open Government National Action Plan for the United States of America."

4. "Communiqué sur la Conférence Internationale sur la Participation Citoyenne et Budgets Participatifs en Afrique."

5. Travaline, "Clinton tells marketers we live in a Participation Age . . . "

6. Lee, McQuarrie, and Walker, *Democratizing inequalities*, 7.

7. Fung, "Putting the public back into governance," 514.

8. Mansuri and Rao, *Localizing development*. Cited in Fung, "Putting the public back into governance," 514.

9. National League of Cities, *Making local democracy work*. Godwin explores the data further to show "that a large majority (69 percent) had citizens serve on ad hoc task forces and a fairly high percentage of cities held neighborhood meetings (48 percent) and town meetings (39 percent)" (Godwin, "Civic engagement and fiscal stress in American cities," 253).

10. Recent research in Southern Europe highlights that most municipalities "have developed considerable participatory activity" (Font, Della Porta, and Sintomer, *Participatory democracy in Southern Europe*, 42).

11. Peck and Theodore, "Mobilizing policy."

12. For a fascinating account of the place of participatory democracy in the history of U.S. social movements, see Polletta, "Participatory democracy in the new millennium"; "Awkward movements"; "Social movement cultures."

13. Polletta, "How participatory democracy became white," 275.

14. See, for example, the discussion in Case and Taylor, *Co-ops, communes and collectives*; and for a classic study of the antinuclear movement, see Downey, "Ideology and the clamshell identity."

15. Boyte, *Backyard revolution*.

16. Walker, "Privatizing participation"; Kleine and Von Hauff, "Sustainability-driven implementation of corporate social responsibility." See also Walker and Rea, "Political mobilization of firms and industries."

17. Fung, "Putting the Public Back into Governance," 520.

18. Ibid., 521.

19. Lee, *Do-it-yourself democracy.*

20. Peck and Theodore, "Mobilizing policy."

21. Jasanoff, *Fifth branch.*

22. Lee, McQuarrie, and Walker, *Democratizing inequalities.*

23. Crouch, *Post-democracy.*

24. Brown, *Undoing the demos.*

25. Held, *Prospects for democracy.*

26. Cooke and Kothari, *Participation.*

27. Cleaver, "Paradoxes of participation," 598.

28. Hickey and Mohan, *Participation—From tyranny to transformation?*

29. Leal, "Participation."

30. See Li, "Beyond 'the state' and failed schemes"; Ong, *Neoliberalism as exception.*

31. Rose, "Death of the social?" 330.

32. Ferguson, *Anti-politics machine.*

33. Rancière, *Future of the image,* 78.

34. Brown, *Undoing the demos,* 2.

35. Keck and Sikkink, *Activists beyond borders.*

36. Babb, "Social consequences of structural adjustment."

37. Evans, "Counterhegemonic globalization."

38. Crozier, Huntington, and Watanuki, *Crisis of democracy.*

39. See Goldfrank, "World Bank and the globalization of participatory budgeting."

40. See Fung and Wright, "Deepening democracy."

41. Ferguson, *Give a man a fish,* 2.

42. Ibid., 1.

43. Ibid., 171.

44. Ibid., 67.

45. Mosse, "Anti-social anthropology?"

46. For example, in addition to Mosse's book on development there is also Carothers, *Assessing democracy assistance.*

47. In addition to the observations and interviews, both authors also worked on—and actively promoted—participatory budgeting in different capacities over the years. Gianpaolo was one of the founders of the Participatory Budgeting Project described in Chapter 5 and assisted the alderman on a volunteer basis. Ernesto is one of the founders of Antigona, a collective that assists the implementation of participatory projects in Spain, and worked on

Córdoba's participatory budget as an employee of city hall. Nicole Summers, our coauthor for Chapter 5, was a staffer in the ward office. As we have mentioned, we very much subscribe to the view that the traditional division between "field" and "desk" does not hold for many of us whose professional work continues to engage the relevant communities. However this does not mean there are no potential ethical pitfalls in these entanglements. All of the evidence in this book only comes from open, public meetings, published statements, and formal, explicit interviews. We do not include any identifying details about individuals other than for elected officials.

48. There are many excellent works by the likes of Tania Li, Aiwah Ong, and slightly earlier, James Marcus, in anthropology, who make the case for various versions of what we think of as ethnographies of circulation. In sociology, in a slightly different register, scholars like Leslie Selziger, Millie Thayer (global ethnography), and Michael Burawoy make a case for micro interactions in global structures.

49. Peck and Theodore, "Mobilizing policy."

50. Preston, Cooper, and Coombs, "Fabricating budgets," 564.

51. Ginzburg, *Clues, myths, and the historical method.*

52. Peck, "Cities beyond compare?" 160.

53. Ibid., 172.

54. In fairness, many civil society theorists such as Habermas and Fraser recognize this problem but generally deal with it at a very high level of abstraction.

55. This is certainly true of our own earlier work. See Baiocchi, "Participation, politics, and activism," as a prime example. This is also true of very many subsequent studies on participatory budgeting.

56. Purcell, "Urban democracy and the local trap."

57. Peck, "Cities beyond compare?" 172.

58. Lascoumes and Le Gales, "Introduction: Understanding public policy through its instruments," 10.

59. Hetland, "The crooked line"; Wampler and McNulty, "Does participatory governance Matter?; Font, Della Porta, and Sintomer, *Participatory democracy in Southern Europe*; Goldfrank, "The World Bank and the globalization of participatory budgeting."

60. Latour, *Science in action*, 29. Similarly scholars of diffusion have argued that a program which seems appealing on a surface level "attracts disproportionate attention" and is embraced because of "its apparent promise, not its demonstrated effects" (Weyland, *Bounded rationality and policy diffusion*).

61. The definition continues: "It is a particular type of institution, a technical device with the generic purpose of carrying a concrete concept of the politics/society relationship and sustained by a concept of regulation" (Lascoumes and Le Gales, "Introduction: Understanding public policy through its instruments," 4).

62. As Lascoumes and Le Gales put it: "landing from heaven" (4).

63. Lascoumes and Le Gales, "Introduction: Understanding public policy through its instruments," 7.

64. See Laclau and Mouffe, *Hegemony and socialist strategy*; Mouffe, *Democratic paradox*; and Laclau, *On populist reason*.

65. Rancière, *Aux bords du politique*.

Chapter Two: The New Spirit of Government

1. See, for example, the account in Julian Brash's *Bloomberg's New York*.

2. "Talking Transition," Open Society Foundations.

3. Chris Smith, "Q&A."

4. Kaplan, "Coalition seeks public's advice on New York City's goals."

5. Ratner, "New Yorkers are holding a great participatory policy-making conference."

6. NYT Editorial Board, "Leave an idea, take an idea."

7. "Mayor-elect Bill de Blasio on Talking Transition," YouTube.

8. Chris Smith, "Q&A."

9. Nam, "Suggesting frameworks of citizen-sourcing via Government 2.0."

10. Rancière goes on to argue that exercises in partition of the sensible presuppose "a partition between what is visible and what is not, of what can be heard from the inaudible." Certain kinds of claims or logic of claims are thus rendered invisible. Rancière, "Ten theses on politics."

11. Wright, *Envisioning real utopias*; Sintomer, Herzberg, and Röcke, "Démocratie participative et modernisation des services publics"; Saward, "Making democratic connections."

12. David Scott, *Conscripts of modernity*, 4.

13. Ibid., 5.

14. Boltanski and Chiapello, *New spirit of capitalism*, 57. They focus on arguments and justifications for new techniques because they believe these to have a performative power—they "aim to bring about what they represent as actual."

15. Schumpeter, *Capitalism, socialism and democracy*.

16. Przeworski, *Democracy and the limits of self-government*.

17. Bell, *Power, influence, and authority*.

18. Offe, "Social protection in a supranational context."

19. Bobbio, *Future of democracy*.

20. As Roberts says, "Direct deliberative citizen engagement is likely to be used to the extent that there is dissatisfaction with current government policy and procedures; the higher the level of dissatisfaction, the more likely that direct citizen engagement will be employed as a mechanism to reduce dissatisfaction levels" (Roberts, "Public deliberation in an age of direct citizen participation," 343).

21. Hood, "Public management for all seasons?"

22. O'Toole, *Ideal of public service*, 6.

23. Dunleavy et al., "New public management is dead."

24. Organisation for Economic Co-operation and Development, "Annual Report 2003."

25. Duneleavey and Hood, "From old public administration to new public management."

26. Denhardt and Denhardt, "New public service," 551.

27. There are several accounts of the clash. See Cratz, *Battle for Gotham*.

28. Osborne and Gaebler, " Reinventing government."

29. Harvey, *Urban experience*, 37–38.

30. Sheppard and Leitner, "*Quo vadis* neoliberalism?" 186.

31. Harvey, *Brief history of neoliberalism*.

32. Particularly useful are the excellent new works exploring just this conjuncture. Among them are Lee, McQuarrie, and Walker, *Democratizing inequalities;* Walker, *Grassroots for hire*; and McQuarrie, "No contest."

33. Crenson and Ginsberg, *Downsizing democracy.*

34. Vigoda and Golembiewski, "Citizenship behavior and the spirit of new managerialism," 275.

35. Castells, *City and the grassroots*; Borja, *Descentralización política y participación*; Sirianni and Friedland, *Civic innovation in America*.

36. Crenson and Ginsberg, *Downsizing democracy.*

37. Leal, "Participation"; Crenson and Ginsberg, *Downsizing democracy*; Cook and Kothari, *Participation*; Cleaver, "Paradoxes of participation"; Eliasoph, *Avoiding politics*; James Ferguson, *Anti-politics machine*.

38. Osborne and Gaebler, "Reinventing government."

39. The other three principles were "Cutting red tape"; "Empowering employees to get results"; and "Cutting government back to basics" (Clark, "Reinventing government").

40. James Thompson, "Reinvention as reform."

41. Sirianni and Friedland, *Civic innovation in America*; Boyte, *Backyard revolution.*

42. Daniel Ferguson, "Understanding horizontal governance"; Swyngedouw, "Impossible sustainability and the post-political condition"; Crenson and Ginsberg, *Downsizing democracy*; Crouch, *Post-democracy.*

43. Pitkin, *Concept of representation*; Sartori, *Social science concepts*; Lasch, "Politics of nostalgia."

44. Crenson and Ginsberg, *Downsizing democracy*, 234.

45. Pharr, Putnam, and Dalton, "Quarter-century of declining confidence."

46. Bobbio, *Future of democracy*.

47. Bryson, Crosby, and Bloomberg, "Public value governance," 445. Cited in Denhardt and Denhardt, "New public service revisited."

48. Leighninger, *Next form of democracy*, 4.

49. Craig, *Malevolent leaders*; Tolchin, *Angry American*; Nye, Zelikow, and King, *Why people don't trust government*; Pharr and Putnam, *Disaffected democracies*.

50. Ansolabehere and Iyengar, *Going negative*, 2.

51. Stivers, *Culture of cynicism*; Cappella and Jamieson, *Spiral of cynicism*; Chaloupka, *Everybody knows*; Purdy, "After apathy."

52. Bellah et al., *Habits of the heart*; Goldfarb, *Cynical society*; Wuthnow, "United States"; Toqueville, *Democracy in America, 627.*

53. Almond and Verba, *Political attitudes and democracy in five nations*; Inglehart, "Renaissance of political culture."

54. Keane, *Life and death of democracy.*

55. Magnier, "Between institutional learning and re-legitimization"; Kersting and Vetter, *Reforming local government in Europe.*

56. Font, Della Porta, and Sintomer, *Participatory democracy in Southern Europe*; Colino and Del Pino, "Un fantasma recorre Europa"; Milner, "Urban governance and local democracy in France."

57. National League of Cities, "National municipal policy and resolutions."

58. Sirianni and Friedland, *Civic innovation in America, 231.*

59. Ansell and Gash, "Collaborative governance in theory and practice"; Stoker, "Public value management."

60. Stoker, "Public value management," 42.

61. Bingham, Nabatchi, and O'Leary, "New governance," 551.

62. Borraz and John, "Transformation of urban political leadership in Western Europe."

63. Box, *Citizen governance, 231.*

64. Ibid., 161.

65. Organisation for Economic Co-operation and Development, "Governance in the 21st Century," 7.

66. Stoker, "Public value management."

67. Fattore, Dubois, and Lapenta, "Measuring new public management and governance in political debate."

68. Graham Smith, "Revitalising politics through democratic innovation?"

69. National League of Cities, *Making local democracy work.*

70. Council of Europe, Committee of Ministers, "Participation of citizens in local public life."

71. Birch, "Public participation in local government"; Sintomer and de Maillard, "Limits to local participation and deliberation in the French 'politique de la ville'"; Graham Smith, *Democratic innovations*; Ganuza and Francés, *El círculo virtuoso de la democracia.*

72. Roussopoulos and Benello, *Participatory democracy.*

73. Newton, "Curing the democratic malaise with democratic innovations";

Geissel, "Impact of democratic innovations in Europe"; Graham Smith, *Democratic innovations*; Saward, "Enacting democracy."

74. Inglehart, *Culture shift in advanced industrial society*; *Modernization and postmodernization*; Dalton, *Democratic challenges, democratic choices.*

75. "OIDP distinction, 'Best Practice in Citizen Participation.'"

76. According to the project description, information is gathered from villagers and projects are vetted for adequacy (the description of the project specifically gives the example of "share the funds in cash evenly for every household" as an ineligible idea); a council of elected village representatives votes on which projects to develop, before undertaking a process of implementation and monitoring: "build a new balance between individual rights and collective cohesion"; "secure a medium-term loan"; "make rural public investment much more transparent"; "social inclusion of the Chengdu participatory budgeting remains one of the challenges"; "building liberal institutions within an illiberal polity."

77. Graham Smith, *Democratic innovations.*

78. Newton, "Curing the democratic malaise with democratic innovations"; Geissel, "Impact of democratic innovations in Europe"; Sintomer, Herzberg, and Röcke, "Démocratie participative et modernisation des services publics."

79. Geissel, "Impact of Democratic innovations in Europe," 164.

80. Ibid., 170.

81. Ganuza and Francés, "Deliberative turn in participation"; Sintomer, Herzberg, and Röcke, "Démocratie participative et modernisation des services publics"; Wampler, "Can participatory institutions promote pluralism?"

82. Ganuza, Nez, and Morales, "Struggle for a voice"; Baiocchi, Heller, and Silva, *Bootstrapping democracy*; Talpin, *Schools of democracy*; Sintomer, Herzberg, and Röcke, *Démocratie participative et modernisation des services publics.*

83. Landemore, "Deliberation, cognitive diversity, and democratic inclusiveness"; Sintomer, *Petite histoire de l'expérimentation démocratique.*

84. Lang, "Citizen learning in state-sponsored institutions."

85. Barabas, "How deliberation affects policy opinions."

86. Manin, Stein, and Mansbridge describe it succinctly: "We need not argue that individuals, when they begin to deliberate political matters, know nothing of what they want. They know what they want in part: they have certain preferences and some information, but these are unsure, incomplete, often confused and opposed to one another. The process of deliberation, the confrontation of various points of view, helps to clarify information and to sharpen their own preferences. They may even modify their initial objectives" ("On legitimacy and political deliberation," 351).

87. As Manin, Stein, and Mansbridge note, "We must affirm, at the risk of contradicting a long tradition, that legitimate law is the *result of general deliberation*, and not the *expression of the general will*" (ibid., 352).

88. Swyngedouw, "Governance innovation and the citizen."

89. Skocpol, *Diminished democracy*, 25.

90. Pinçon and Pinçon-Charlot, "Sociologia da alta burguesia"; Gittel et al., *Limits to citizen participation*; Verba, Schlozman, and Brady, *Voice and equality*.

91. Norris, Walgrave, and van Aelst, "Does protest signify disaffection?"

92. Micheletti and Stolle, *Politics, products, and markets*.

93. Young, "Communication and the other."

94. Boltanski and Chiapello, *New spirit of capitalism*.

95. Epstein, *Political protest and cultural revolution*, 40.

96. "Port Huron Statement of the Students for a Democratic Society," 1.

97. The authorities' reactions to the 1960s led to an almost obsessive creation of consultative institutions at the municipal level. These structures were a long way from participatory theory and permitted articulations of discontent rather than real political expression. See Skocpol, *Diminished democracy*; McQuarrie, "No contest"; Jordan and Maloney, *Protest business?*

98. Castells, *City and the grassroots*; Sirianni and Friedland, *Civic innovation in America*; Epstein, *Political protest and cultural revolution*.

99. Pleyers, *Alter-globalization*.

100. Boltanski and Thevenot, *De la justification*.

101. Chris Smith, "Talking transition survey tells de Blasio's tale of two cities."

102. "Bill de Blasio," Decide NYC.

103. "Mayor de Blasio announces the launch of the national 'Cities for Citizenship' effort."

104. Rancière, *Aux bords du politique*, 11-12.

105. Mouffe, *Democratic paradox*; Crouch, *Post-democracy*; Rancière, *La haine de la démocratie*.

Chapter Three: The Global Spread of Participation

1. Interview with Brian Levy at World Bank, Washington, DC, June 2010.

2. Tenants and Workers United, "Projects."

3. Living wage campaigns seek to enact local ordinances that increase the minimum wage for public contracts to a level more appropriate to local cost of living. Alexandria, Virginia, adopted its ordinance in 2000. See Luce (2005).

4. Right to the City Alliance, "Right to the City charter."

5. Offe, "Governance"; Brenner, Peck, and Theodore, "Variegated neoliberalization."

6. Ong, *Neoliberalism as exception*.

7. Melo and Baiocchi, "Deliberative democracy and local governance."

8. Strange and Tooze, *International politics of surplus capacity*.

9. We thank Marcelo K. Silva for turning up this reference and for long insisting that the Workers' Party did not invent participatory budgeting.

10. Here we cover the same terrain, though avoiding what sometimes in the history of ideas is called "Whig history"—the telling of events that presents history as a series of progressive successes, ignoring controversies, reversals, failed ideas, and dead-ends (Mayr, "When is historiography Whiggish?").

11. Uniao das Associaçoes de Moradores de Porto Alegre (UAMPA), "Conselhos minicipais."

12. Ibid.

13. The center of the diagram reads: "Forum of Debates in the Neighborhood. Associations or *Conselhos* in the Community." The sides of the diagram read: "Mother's Clubs. Church Councils. Sports Clubs. Others. Associations. Service Clubs. Parent-Teacher Associations."

14. In terms of political theory it is the difference between associational democracy (or corporatism for that matter) and direct democracy; the difference between placing special value in autonomous spaces in civil society and their capacity to generate demands, and placing special value in spaces where all citizens can participate on equal footing. For example, see Cohen and Rogers, "*Associations and democracy.*"

15. Gildo Lima, of the administration, recalled that "the party comes, basically, from the university students' movement, and of some sectors of the union movement, . . . the bank-tellers' syndicate, civil servants, etc., and therefore *with little popular basis.* To be honest we know that this basis in fact in town is the PDT. This party, with its populist contradictions, is a party rooted in Porto Alegre; I'm convinced of it" (Lima, "*Uma aventura responsavel,*" 58). An activist recalled, "A lot of us left the movement to come work for the administration and we later realized this was a mistake because then the PDT became hegemonic in some areas" (Marlene, interview in Porto Alegre, May 8, 1998). Another one suggested, "It was a practical question because the administration needed people, and one after the other, everyone who was a community leader left" (Zé Carlos, interview in Porto Alegre, June 10, 1998).

16. Genro, "Licoes da intervencao," 57.

17. To the question whether this represented a rupture with union allies, Genro responded in the same interview that "this was not a severing, because there would have had to be an alliance. . . . The administration does not establish alliances with unions. That is a completely distorted vision" (Genro, "Licoes da intervencao,"58).

18. Roughly at the same time, some within the party attempted to create a "Popular Council"—"an instrument of popular mobilization"—in one of the city's remote districts, which could serve as a "voice of the people" with the new administration. The outcome was considered a failure because "activists

replicated clientelistic patterns" by electing one of the local "bosses" to the head of the *conselho*.

19. Iria Sharão, one of the architects of the process, recalled this in an interview with Mara Harnecker (Harnecker, *Brasil, la alcaldía de Porto Alegre*, 22). Other recollections from the time, such as the ones recorded by Fedozzi in *Orçamento participativo*, offer similar interpretations.

20. For example, one of the early but discarded versions proposed that the Council of the Budget include six seats set aside for "class associations," including a seat for the national labor federation as well as one for the local municipal employees' union (Prefeitura Municipal de Porto Alegre, "Conselho Municipal do Plano de Governo e Orçamento").

21. Pont, "Porto Alegre, e a luta pela democracia."

22. Pont cites the referendum in Switzerland or participatory traditions from the Middle Ages in Europe as existing traditions.

23. Certainly it became impossible to access funds, investments, or city projects outside of the participatory process.

24. Navarro, "'Participatory budgeting,'" 26.

25. This is often what is described as happening in administrations that introduce new public management.

26. Prefeitura Municipal de Porto Alegre, "Proceso de avaliaçao da gestao da Frente Popular."

27. Real estate taxes became increasingly important, going from 5.8% of the volume of municipal revenues to nearly 18% of total revenues, while the services tax went on to account for 20% of municipal revenues (Santos, *Democracia e participação*, 68). Tax evasion was also significantly reduced over ten years (Baeirle, "La experiencia brasileña en el Presupuesto Participativo").

28. Santos, *Democracia e participação*; Bremaeker, *Panorama das finanças municipais em 2003*.

29. Interview with one of the founders of Uniao das Associaçoes de Moradores de Porto Alegre (UAMPA), August 21, 2008.

30. Ibid.

31. Interview with one of the leaders of Uniao das Associaçoes de Moradores de Porto Alegre (UAMPA), conducted on August 10, 2008.

32. "We do not believe in this type of classic representation; for example, so and so is representative of the bank-tellers union and goes there to the PB; that is not true, he is representing himself and his will because all the bank-tellers are not going to meet and deliberate on a position for him to carry . . . and this is why we work with direct citizenship and not associations" (Lima, "A experiencia da prefeitura de Porto Alegre," 122).

33. Fórum Nacional de Participação Popular (FNPP), *Experiências de orçamento participativo no Brasil*, 2.

34. Wampler and Avritzer, "Spread of participatory budgeting in Brazil," 37–52.

35. Lima Figueiredo and Lamounier, *As cidades que dão certo.*

36. Jacobi, "Movimentos sociais"; Jacobi, *Politicas socias e ampliação da cidadania.*

37. Genro and de Souza, *Orcamento participativo.* Translated into French in 1998 (*Quand les habitants gérent vraiment leur ville. Le budget participative: L'experience de Porto Alegre au Brésil,* Paris: Editions Charles Léopold Meyer) and into Spanish in 2000 (*El Presupuesto Participativo: La experiencia de Porto Alegre,* Barcelona: Serbal).

38. UN-Habitat, "Habitat agenda goals and principles."

39. Oliveira, "embaixadores da participação." One concern had been that administrators in the Workers' Party not be seen as a parochial, leftist party out of touch with global trends. Other political parties were capitalizing on this, presenting themselves as modernizers. From 1996 an "international relations" department was instituted within the administration, closely linked with the operation of participatory budgeting. Top administrators sought out international, high-profile visits to promote the "Workers' Party way of governing" and in particular PB. The Porto Alegre administration during this period regularly received visitors from administrators from other cities and dispatched its own functionaries to other cities. In interviews with members of the Office of Community Relations and the Planning Office some recalled taking *dozens* of international trips a year in the early 2000s. Much of this is documented in the important work of Osmany Porto de Oliveira and Vanessa Marx.

40. Marx, *Las ciudades internacionales.*

41. Blackburn and Holland argue in the introduction to their collection *Who Changes?* that twenty-nine distinct participatory methodologies have been developed since the 1970s. The World Bank, for example, since the 1970s has deployed "beneficiary assessment," "social analysis," and "participatory rural appraisal" methodologies in the crafting of "Poverty Reduction Strategy Papers" (Francis, "Participatory development at the World Bank"). Participatory rural appraisal, as described by Chambers in *Rural Development,* seeks to "enable poor people to express and analyze the realities of their lives and conditions and themselves to plan, monitor and evaluate their actions."

42. World Bank Staff, *World development report 1997.*

43. The *World Development Report* of 2006 is entitled *Empowerment* and devotes many pages to participatory budgeting in particular. The slightly earlier *World Bank Participation Sourcebook* (1996) for example, defines several participatory methodologies and presumed benefits from incorporating participation in development programs, such as increased effectiveness, sustainability, and legitimacy for interventions.

44. Organisation for Economic Co-operation and Development, *Citizens as partners*.

45. Cleaver, "Paradoxes of participation," 597.

46. Goldsmith, "Is governance reform a catalyst for development?"

47. Sintomer, Herzberg, and Allegretti, *Learning from the South*, 25.

48. Between the U.N.-sponsored programs, the blurrily defined networks coalescing around the World Social Forum, and the EU programs, an international network of practitioner-experts began to come together around participatory budgeting in the early 2000s. The same dozen or so principal experts circulated between all of these settings, sometimes seeing each other several times a year. Nonetheless this group came together around different projects that sometimes mobilized millions of dollars. The EU program with Latin America local governments (URB-AL) was one particularly important setting, especially its "Network-9," dedicated to PB and launched in 2003. There was also significant transit between the academic world and this new group of experts. Several of the reports published on PB were based on academic work. The first master's and doctorate on PB were written at the Federal University in Porto Alegre in the mid-1990s but were soon followed by literally hundreds more throughout Brazil and later Europe and the United States. Some of the more prominent names in the world of PB expertise got their start by doing doctoral fieldwork on PB, while others, after working on participatory budgeting in the Porto Alegre administration, returned to graduate school to reflect on these experiences. Some of the experts came from the academy, and favorable scholarship on participatory budgeting played an important legitimating role in this early international travel. See also Oliveira, "Embaixadores."

49. Ramonet, "Promise of Porto Alegre"; Oliveira, "Embaixadores."

50. Ibid.

51. In the course of our research we examined fifty-four such toolkits. While this analysis does not substitute for the fieldwork we describe in later chapters, we concur with Boltanski and Chiapello (*New spirit of capitalism*), who find instructional manuals especially telling.

52. They typically provide a concise history of participatory budgeting's origins and a brief discussion of its political or social merits. This promotional element however is secondary to their primary purpose as implementation guides for potential promoters. Some (UN-Habitat's *Africa Toolkit, Volume 2*, of 2008, is a formidable example) even include template documents to be used while running a participatory budgeting process, such as sample surveys of citizen interests, budget allocation schematics, and self-assessment questions, summarizing key issues to which readers should pay particular attention.

53. www.thepeoplesbudget.org.uk/makethecase/conservative/ (accessed May 16, 2012)

54. Allegretti and Herzberg, "Participatory budgets in Europe."

55. A good overview on European experiences is in Sintomer, Herzberg, and Röcke, "Démocratie participative et modernisation des services publics"; and Sintomer, Herzberg, and Allegretti, *Learning from the South.*

56. For example, the comparative study coordinated by Sintomer, Herzberg, and Röcke proposed a methodological definition, according to which the participatory budgets are processes characterized by the presence of five elements: (1) the financial or budgetary dimension is explicitly discussed; (2) they are organized at least at the city level or that of a decentralized district that corresponds to an elective institutional level (a neighborhood council or investment fund would not be a participatory budget); (3) they are repeated processes (a single meeting, an isolated referendum on budgetary subjects would not be a participatory budget); (4) they have to include a certain form of public deliberation (closed meetings of sectoral councils would not be participatory budgets, nor would a survey about what citizens think about the budget); and (5) they need a dimension of accountability regarding the results of the process, providing feedback on implementation of codecided public works. Sintomer, Herzberg, Röcke, "Démocratie participative et modernisation des services publics."

57. Sintomer, Herzberg, and Allegretti, *Learning from the South*; He, "Civic engagement through participatory budgeting in China."

58. It is clearly very difficult to estimate this number with any precision. Our rough estimate comes from a combination of interviews and internet-based research. A more precise estimate would require answering several questions about any one place, such as whether the process is ongoing or meets some minimum requirements; it would also require deciding whether to count PB processes that are entirely outside of governments (such as within a university student council budget). Our number is intended to capture municipal governments and assumes anything that calls itself PB "counts." Our estimate is in line with other estimates, such as Peck and Theodore, *Fast policy*; Sintomer, Herzberg, and Röcke, "Démocratie participative et modernisation des services publics"; and Oliveira, "Embaixadores."

59. Peck and Theodore, "Mobilizing policy."

60. Wolfowitz, "Good governance and development," 3.

61. Interview with Shah, August 3, 2009, World Bank, Washington, DC.

62. Policy instruments in this way "are not neutral devices: they produce specific effects, independently of the objective pursued (the aims ascribed to them), which structure public policy according to their own logic" (Lascoumes and Le Gales, "Introduction: Understanding public policy through its instruments," 3).

Chapter Four:
The Rhetoric of Emancipation

1. Interview with the former councilor in citizen participation in Córdoba, April 27, 2009.

2. Castells, *City and the grassroots*. See also Alfonso, *Espacio político del movimiento vecinal*; García Fernández and González Ruiz, *Presente y futuro de las asociaciones de vecinos*; Guerrero, *Veinte años de encuentros y desencuentros de las asociaciones de vecinos;* and Villasante, *Los vecinos en la calle*. For Córdoba, see Dios Mellado and Juliá, *Memoria de la transición democrática en Córdoba;* Legrán, *El movimiento ciudadano andaluz en la democracia*; Rosa, *La estación de Córdoba*; and Contreras-Becerra, "El movimiento vecinal en Andalucía durante el tardofranquismo y el proceso de cambio político."

3. Villasante, "Las democracias participativas."

4. Sintomer, Herzberg, and Röcke, "Démocratie participative et modernisation des services publics." There is of course some dispute about both claims about Córdoba and Chicago. There are references to other prior attempts in both the United States and Europe, such as an attempted participatory budgeting process in Portland, Oregon. For our purposes, however, these other fleeting experiences did not succeed nor did they have any influence on subsequent experiences.

5. Insofar as political parties were banned, neighborhood associations formed the only legitimate channel through which citizens could face the regime's authorities. Much of the political resistance to the dictatorship took refuge in neighborhood associations.

6. Julia Anguita was the first mayor. Later on he would be the national leader of the same political organization in the 1990s.

7. Aguiar and Navarro. "Democracia y participación ciudadana en los municipios."

8. Font, *Ciudadanos y decisiones públicas*.

9. Ruiz, *Por un modelo público de agua*, 70.

10. He went on to say, "[The new mechanisms] have undermined the associations' legitimacy by assuming that an association is no longer needed because there are people involved in every neighborhood, because the politicians prefer to speak directly to the inhabitants rather than to intermediaries, who will always tend to detract from their power."

11. Interview with the president of the Federation of Neighborhood Associations, in Córdoba, April 27, 2007.

12. Sintomer, Herzberg, and Röcke, *Démocratie participative et modernisation des services publics*.

13. Ibid., 87–89.

14. "In Cordoba, the combination of strong-willed top-down, institutional actors and bottom-up citizen engagement allowed PB to build upon existing participatory traditions and genuinely transform the urban agendas—even if for a short period of time, and to a limited extent." Kębłowski and Van Criekingen, "How 'alternative' alternative urban policies really are?"

15. Ganuza, "Les origines des budgets participatif."

16. Nez and Ganuza, "Among militants and deliberative laboratories."

17. Interview with Pablo Soto, June 17, 2015. Accessed September 2015. www .diagonalperiodico.net/global/27006-estamos-revolucion-democratica.html.

Chapter Five:
A Government Closer to the People

1. Nyden, Figert, Shibley, and Burrows, *Building community.*

2. Berrey, "Divided over Diversity."

3. Burke, *Racial ambivalence in diverse communities.*

4. Nyden, Maly, and Lukehart, "Emergence of stable racially and ethnically diverse urban communities"; Maly and Leachman, "Rogers Park, Edgewater, Uptown, and Chicago Lawn, Chicago."

5. Leachman, Nyden, Peterman, and Coleman, *Black, White, and Shades of Brown.*

6. Molotch, *Managed Integration.*

7. Berrey, "Divided over Diversity," 149.

8. The Participatory Budgeting Project, or PBP, later became a nonprofit.

9. Latour, *Science in action.*

10. Murray, "Regulating activism."

11. See Weber, Crum, and Salinas, "Civics of community development," 273.

12. Ibid.

13. Bae, "Participatory democracy in Chicago."

14. This event is carefully described in Baiocchi, Bennett, Cordner, Klein, and Savell, *Civic imagination.*

15. The Great Cities Institute and the Chicago Community Trust assisted in creating a citywide steering committee. For the 2012–13 cycle three other aldermen implemented PB processes in two neighborhoods in the northern part of Chicago (Wards 45 and 46), representing Portage Park and Uptown, and one in the south (Ward 5), and South Shore/Greater Grand Crossing.

16. A tenant's rights group active among public housing residents—Community Voices Heard—had expressed some interest in it after hearing of its successful use in Toronto's public housing, and then of its implementation in Chicago. In connection with the two cochairs of New York City's Progressive Caucus in the city council, and the outside assistance of the Participatory Budget Project, they led this initiative.

17. Cited in Jabola-Carolus, "Injecting democracy into public spending."

18. See, for example, Katinas, "Menchaca's goal: 'I want to be part of a movement.'"

19. That first rulebook stipulated that attendance to assemblies would be open to anyone regardless of immigration status who is sixteen and over, who

resides, works, or studies in the area. Voting on projects was originally limited to those eighteen and over; voting age was then lowered to sixteen, and in some districts to fourteen.

20. There are too many to list, but for a sample see Katinas, "Menchaca's goal: 'I want to be part of a movement'"; Gilman, "Innovation is not just apps"; Su, "'Whose budget? Our budget?"

21. See the account in Davidson and Kutz, "Grassroots austerity."

22. Cited in Cha, "Vallejo, Calif., once bankrupt, is now a model for cities in an age of austerity."

23. *Times-Herald* staff, "Two Vallejo participatory budgeting assemblies remain," *Times Herald Online*, March 4, 2015. Accessed October 1, 2015. www.timesheraldonline.com/general-news/20150304/two-vallejo-participatory-budgeting-assemblies-remain

24. www.csus.edu/PPA/thesis-project/bank/2013/Chapin.pdf. Participedia.

25. See, for example, Isaac Jabola-Carolus's piece in Occupy.com, "Injecting democracy into public spending."

26. Vallejo's process is nearly identical but began in May and ended in October in the past.

27. See, for example, Castillo, "Reflections on participatory budgeting in New York City"; or Linnell Ajello, "Participatory budgeting swells, and so do questions about impact," citylimits.org, July 2, 2015. Accessed October 1, 2015. http://citylimits.org/2015/07/02/participatory-budgeting-swells-and-so-do-questions-about-impact/

28. See, for example, Stephen Choi, "Redefining citizenship," *Huffington Post,* September 15, 2015.

29. For year one, see Kasdan, Markman, and Covey, "People's Budget."

30. In one district the "very poor" made up nearly a fourth of participants, despite being only 8% of the population. Half of overall participants had never been involved in community issues. See the various reports published by the Urban Justice Center, all available online for careful discussion of the patterns of inclusion in PB across New York. See Kasdan, Markman, and Covey, "People's Budget."

31. Stewart, Miller, Hildreth, and Wright-Phillips, "Participatory budgeting in the United States."

32. Latino residents make up one-fourth of the population in the ward. In the 2013 survey they made up 6% of neighborhood assembly participants and none of the community reps. Whites, who make up 39% of the population, made up more than three-fourths of the community reps and nearly two-thirds of the assembly participants. See Weber, Crum, and Salinas, "Civics of community development."

33. Ibid., 273.

34. Ibid., 272.

35. Ajello, "Participatory budgeting swells, and so do questions about impact."

36. Ibid.

37. Though home to just 73,000 residents, it has fifty-three industrial facilities and six coal-mining plants in addition to the diesel pollution from the heavy truck traffic on the bridge. In 2009 one study found that some pollutants were present in the air at levels seventy-five times higher than government guidelines. The Clean Air Coalition (CAC) of Western New York, a group of community activists, has been leading these and several other campaigns against polluters. www.cacwny.org/about/our-history/

38. It's important to note that in the years preceding this government decision, activists constantly referenced participatory budgeting. http://whatsnew-buffalo.com/post/63372327082/participatory-budgeting-bringing-democracy-to-Tonawanda

39. http://artvoice.com/issues/v12n40/cover_story

40. Their second choice was an environmental health institute, while funding for a health study came in third. Other projects included creating a tree farm, initiating a relocation fund, and developing a worker toxic exposure education program.

41. www.kentonbee.com/news/2013-06-26/Local_News/Voters_choose_pollution_prevention_as_top_project.html?print=1

42. Ibid.

Chapter Six: The Utopian Undercurrent of Participation

1. Brown, "We are all democrats now," 56.

2. Eggers, *Government 2.0*; Briggs, *Democracy as problem solving*.

3. The distinction is developed in Fraser, "Rethinking the public sphere."

4. Thompson, "Battle for Necropolis."

5. Wedeen, *Ambiguities of domination*.

6. Castoriadis, "Radical imagination and the social instituting imaginary,"136; see also *Imaginary institution of society*.

7. Rancière, *Aux bords du politique*, 43. Italics added.

8. Fung and Wright, *Deepening democracy*.

9. During PB meetings and forums in Porto Alegre, researchers took careful counts of the gender balance of speakers and to what extent we were in the presence of an equal space where anyone could talk or had a voice, but we did not keep a record of how often technical criteria countermanded popular decisions. Most research is participant centered and views the process as participants might: paying closer attention to one's neighbors and proximate others (like facilitators) than government machinery. This is seen in Baiocchi,

"Participation, politics, and activism," and is also found in many subsequent studies on participatory budgeting. It is our belief that the proliferation of PB projects calls for a more nuanced analysis beyond merely investigating meeting rules and counting participants.

10. Baiocchi, Teixeira, and Braaten, "Transformation institutionalized?"; Grazia and de Torres Ribeiro, *Orçamento participativo no Brasil*; Avritzer, *Participatory institutions in democratic Brazil*; Wampler, "Can participatory institutions promote pluralism?"

11. Avritzer, "New public spheres in Brazil"; Baiocchi, *Militants and citizens*; Fedozzi, *Orçamento participativo*.

12. Mouffe, *Return of the political*.

13. Urbinati, *Democracy disfigured*, 30.

14. This has been a frequent criticism of the way that deliberative processes work. See Young, "Communication and the other"; Bohman, "Deliberative democracy and effective social freedom."

15. Rosanvallon, *Democratic legitimacy*; Urbinati, *Democracy disfigured*; Dalton, *Democratic challenges*; Norris, *Democratic deficit*.

16. Most research on new participatory devices unveils the same bias when analyzing who participates in public processes such as PB or public assemblies. Participants are usually white, educated, and better off. But bias is limited in the debate dynamics. Bryan, *Real democracy*; Ganuza and Francés, "Le défi participatif."

17. Habermas, *Between facts and norms*.

18. Urbinati, "Competing for liberty."

19. Habermas describes the pragmatic conditions of communication in a number of works. We recommend one of his later works because he tries to answer criticisms and is especially clear about them. Habermas, *Between naturalism and religion*, ch. 3, 77–97.

20. Dennis Thompson, "Deliberative democratic theory and empirical political science"; Sanders, "Against deliberation."

21. See for example, Cohen and Arato, *Civil society and political theory.*

22. Brazilian administrations are notoriously fragmented, as groups within political parties (or parties themselves) occupy and exert control over particular departments.

23. Navarro, "'Participatory budgeting.'"

24. Baiocchi, *Militants and citizens.*

25. Pont, *Democracia, igualdade e qualidade de vida.*

26. Baiocchi and Ganuza, "Becoming a best practice."

27. Font, Della Porta, and Sintomer, *Participatory democracy in Southern Europe.*

28. Graham Smith, "Revitalising politics through democratic innovation?" 17.

29. Mohan, "Beyond participation."

30. Kothari, "Power, knowledge and social control in participatory development."

31. Ganuza and Francés, *El círculo virtuoso de la democracia*; Sintomer, Herzberg, and Röcke, "Démocratie participative et modernisation des services publics."

32. Graham Smith, *Democratic innovations.*

33. Sintomer, Herzberg, and Allegretti, *Learning from the South,* 8.

34. Baiocchi, Heller, and Silva, *Bootstrapping democracy*; Ganuza and Francés, "Deliberative turn in participation."

35. Ganuza and Francés, "Deliberative turn in participation"; Bassolli, "Participatory budgeting in Italy"; Talpin, *Schools of democracy*; Leubolt, Novy, and Becker, "Changing patterns of participation in Porto Alegre."

36. Baiocchi, Heller, and Silva, *Bootstrapping democracy.*

37. He, "Civic engagement through participatory budgeting in China."

38. Allegretti, "Los presupuestos participativos en África y en Asia."

39. Ganuza and Francés, "Deliberative turn in participation"; Talpin, *Schools of democracy.*

40. Julien Talpin, for example, analyzed the deliberative performance in three European experiences, concluding that they all showed a deficit in argumentative dynamics. He highlighted the lack of plurality, argumentative exchange, and learning. Meanwhile Ernesto Ganuza and Francisco Francés analyzed the problem of inclusion and distribution of deliberative opportunities among participants in eight experiences in Spain. The work unveiled a considerable bias in participation, making it difficult to present a plurality of views in participatory meetings. However, these biases, which overlapped those detected by Talpin (high presence of politicized participants, ideologically akin to the government parties and a demographic profile of middle and upper classes, as in most participatory processes), blur when we consider the distribution of opportunities within deliberative dynamics. Participants, independent of their origin, ideology, profile, or skill, are equally involved in deliberative dynamics, which allows us to suggest that in spite of the argumentative shortcomings, the deliberative context would be accepted by participants and would facilitate their involvement over the differences between them. Talpin suggested that in a noncoercive scenario the deliberation has a chance if conflict is possible, that is, when different beliefs are met. Talpin, *Schools of democracy*; Ganuza and Francés, "Deliberative turn in participation."

41. Law and Mol, "Situating technoscience."

42. Montero, "Experimenting with neoliberalism and democracy."

43. Peck and Theodore, *Fast policy.*

44. Fung, "Putting the public back into governance," 9.

45. Appadurai, "Capacity to aspire."

46. Cited in Jabola-Carolus, "Injecting democracy into public spending."

47. Latino residents make up one-fourth of the population of the ward. In the 2013 survey they made up 6% of neighborhood assembly participants, and none of the community reps. Whites, who make up 39% of the population, made up more than three-fourths of the community reps and nearly two-thirds of the assembly participants. See Weber, Crum, and Salinas, "Civics of community development."

48. Ibid., 272.

49. Latour, *Science in action.*

50. Hay, *Why we hate politics.*

51. Rosanvallon, *Democratic legitimacy.*

52. Lasch, *Revolt of the elites and the betrayal of democracy.*

53. Swyngedouw, "Interrogating post-democratization."

54. Castoriadis, *La societé bureaucratique.*

55. Su, "Between bottom-up and top-down governance."

56. In Berlin the redistricting was driven by the public, which forced the government to hold a referendum in 2011 on this issue. The story is typical of "new public management." In 1999 the Berlin region, with a large public debt, created a PPP (public-private partnership) to manage water and relieve the public coffers. Everything was done under a secret contract, in which the PPP ensured minimal benefit to the two private companies that won the contract. During the early years the price of water increased, employment fell, and investments in infrastructure declined. A citizens' initiative, emulating the popular water councils in Bolivia, launched a campaign calling for a referendum redistricting public contracts. The Berlin government eventually dissolved the PPP a year after the referendum.

Bibliography

Aguiar, Fernando, and Clemente J. Navarro. "Democracia y participación ciudadana en los municipios: ¿Un mercado político de trastos?" *Reis* (2000): 89–III.

Alfonso, C., ed. *Espacio político del movimiento vecinal y del consumerista en la España actual.* Madrid: Fundación de Investigaciones Marxistas, 1987.

Allegretti, Giovanni. "Los presupuestos participativos en África y en Asia." In *Democracia participativa y presupuestos participativos,* ed. Andrés Falck and Pablo Paño. Málaga: Diputación Málaga and Unión Europea, 2011.

———. "Participatory democracies: A slow march toward new paradigms from Brazil to Europe?" 2014. http://classiques.uqac.ca/contemporains/allegretti_giovanni/participatory_democracies/participatory_democracies.pdf

Allegretti, Giovanni, and Carsten Herzberg. *Participatory budgets in Europe: Between efficiency and growing local democracy.* Briefing series 5. Amsterdam: TNI, 2004.

Almond, Gabriel A., and Sidney Verba. *Political attitudes and democracy in five nations.* Boston: Little, Brown, 1965.

Alves, Mariana Lopes, and Giovanni Allegretti. "(In)stability, a key element to understand participatory budgeting: Discussing Portuguese cases." *Journal of Public Deliberation* 8, no. 2 (2012): 3.

Ansell, Chris, and Alison Gash. "Collaborative governance in theory and practice." *Journal of Public Administration Research and Theory* 18, no. 4 (2008): 543–71.

Ansolabehere, Stephen, and Shanto Iyengar. *Going negative: How attack ads shrink and polarize the electorate.* New York: Free Press, 1995.

Appadurai, Arjun. "The capacity to aspire: Culture and the terms of recognition." *Culture and Public Action* (2004): 59–84.

Avritzer, Leonardo. "New public spheres in Brazil: Local democracy and deliberative politics." *International Journal of Urban and Regional Research* 30, no. 3 (2006): 623–37.

———. *Participatory institutions in democratic Brazil.* Baltimore: Johns Hopkins University Press, 2009.

Babb, Sarah. "The social consequences of structural adjustment: Recent evidence and current debates." *Annual Review of Sociology* 31 (2005): 199–222.

Bae, Lena. "Participatory democracy in Chicago: Participatory budgeting is working, important, and going to stay." *Harvard Political Review*, April 2011. http://harvardpolitics.com/united-states/participatory-democracy-in-chicago-participatory-budgeting-is-working-important-and-going-to-stay/

Baierle, Sergio. "La experiencia brasileña en el Presupuesto Participativo: El caso de Porto Alegre." In *Prefectura Municipal Porto Alegre, Financiación local y Presupuesto Participativo, Seminario de lanzamiento, Red 9 URB-AL*, 2003.

Baiocchi, Gianpaolo. *Militants and citizens: The politics of participatory democracy in Porto Alegre*. Stanford, CA: Stanford University Press, 2005.

———. "Participation, politics, and activism: The Porto Alegre experiment and deliberative democratic theory." *Politics and Society* 41 (2001): 43-63.

———. "The Porto Alegre experiment and deliberative democratic theory." *Politics and Society* 29 (2001): 43–72.

Baiocchi, Gianpaolo, Elizabeth Bennett, Alissa Cordner, Peter Klein, and Stephanie Savell. *The civic imagination: Making a difference in American political life*. New York: Routledge, 2014.

Baiocchi, Gianpaolo, and Ernesto Ganuza. "Becoming a best practice: Neoliberalism and the curious case of participatory budgeting." In *Democratizing inequalities: Dilemmas of the new public participation*, ed. Caroline W. Lee, Michael McQuarrie, and Edward T. Walker. New York: New York University Press, 2015.

———. "No parties, no banners: The Spanish experiment with direct democracy." *Boston Review*, January 2012.

Baiocchi, Gianpaolo, Patrick Heller, and Marcelo Kunrath Silva. *Bootstrapping democracy: Transforming local governance and civil society in Brazil*. Stanford, CA: Stanford University Press, 2011.

Baiocchi, Gianpaolo, Ana Claudia Teixeira, and Einar Braaten. "Transformation institutionalized? Making sense of participatory democracy in the Lula era." In *Democratization in the Global South: The importance of transformative politics*, ed. C. Stokke and O. Thornquist. London: Palgrave Macmillan, 2013.

Barabas, Jason. "How deliberation affects policy opinions." *American Political Science Review* 98, no. 4 (2004): 687–701.

Barnes, William, and Bonnie Mann. *Making local democracy work: Municipal officials' views about public engagement*. Washington, DC: National League of Cities, 2010.

Bassolli, Matteo. "Participatory budgeting in Italy: An analysis of (almost democratic) participatory governance arrangements." *International Journal of Urban and Regional Research* (2011). doi: 10.1111/j.1468-2427.2011.01023.x

Bell, David V.J. *Power, influence, and authority: An essay in political linguistics.* Vol. 2. New York: Oxford University Press, 1975.

Bellah, R. N., William M. Sullivan, Steven M. Tipton, Richard Madsen, and Ann Swidler. *Habits of the heart: Individualism and commitment in American life.* Berkeley: University of California Press, 1996.

Berrey, Ellen C. "Divided over diversity: Political discourse in a Chicago neighborhood." *City and Community* 4, no. 2 (2005): 143–70.

Bessette, Joseph. "Deliberative democracy: The majority principle in republican government." *How Democratic Is the Constitution* 102 (1980): 109–11.

Bingham, Lisa Blomgren, Tina Nabatchi, and Rosemary O'Leary. "The new governance: Practices and processes for stakeholder and citizen participation in the work of government." *Public Administration Review* 65, no. 5 (2005): 547–58.

Birch, Demelza. "Public participation in local government: A survey of local authorities." Local and Regional Government Research Unit, ODPM Office of the Deputy Prime Minister, England, 2002.

Blackburn, James, and Jeremy Holland. *Who changes? Institutionalizing participation in development.* Intermediate Technology Publications, 1998.

Bobbio, Noberto. *The future of democracy.* London: Polity Press, 1987.

Bohman, John. "Deliberative democracy and effective social freedom: Capabilities, resources and opportunities." In *Deliberative democracy*, ed. J. Bohman and W. Rehg, 321–48. Cambridge, MA: MIT Press, 1997.

Boltanski, Luc, and Ève Chiapello. *Thex.* Verso: London, 2005.

Boltanski, Luc, and L. Thevenot. *De la justification: Les economies de la grandeur.* Paris: Gallimard, 1991.

Borja, Jordi. *Descentralización política y participación.* Barcelona: PPU, 1988.

Borraz, Olivier, and Peter John. "The transformation of urban political leadership in Western Europe." *International Journal of Urban and Regional Research* 28, no. 1 (2004): 107–20.

Box, Richard C. *Citizen governance: Leading American communities into the 21st century.* Thousand Oaks, CA: Sage, 1997.

Boyte, Harry Chatten. *The backyard revolution: Understanding the new citizen movement.* Philadelphia: Temple University Press, 1980.

Brash, Julian. *Bloomberg's New York: Class and governance in the luxury city.* Athens: University of Georgia Press, 2011.

Bremaeker, F.E.J. *Panorama das finanças municipais em 2003.* Série Estudos Especiais, no. 77. Instituto Brasileiro Administraçao Municipal, 2004.

Brenner, Neil, Jamie Peck, and Nik Theodore. "Variegated neoliberalization: Geographies, modalities, pathways." *Global networks* 10, no. 2 (2010): 182–222.

Briggs, Xavier de Souza. *Democracy as problem solving: Civic capacity in communities across the globe.* Cambridge, MA: MIT Press, 2008.

Brown, Wendy. "We are all democrats now." In *Democracy in what state?* ed. Giorgio Agambe, 44–57. New York: Columbia University Press, 2011.

Brugué, Quim, and Ricard Gomà. "Las políticas públicas locales: Agendas complejas, roles estratégicos y estilo relacional." In *Gobiernos locales y políticas públicas: Bienestar social, promoción económica y territorio.* Ariel, 1998.

Bryan, Frank M. *Real democracy: The New England town meeting and how it works.* Chicago: University of Chicago Press, 2004.

Bryson, John M., Barbara C. Crosby, and Laura Bloomberg. "Public value governance: Moving beyond traditional public administration and the new public management." *Public Administration Review* 74, no. 4 (2014): 445–56.

Buck, Alexy, and Brigitte Geissel. "The education ideal of the democratic citizen in Germany: Challenges and changing trends." *Education, Citizenship and Social Justice* 4, no. 3 (2009): 225–43.

Burke, Meghan. *Racial ambivalence in diverse communities.* Plymouth: Lexington Books, 2012.

Cabannes, Yves. "The impact of participatory budgeting on basic services: Municipal practices and evidence from the field." *Environment and Urbanization* 27, no. 1 (2015): 257–84.

Callon, Michel. "Some elements of a sociology of translation: Domestication of the scallops and the fishermen of St Brieuc Bay." In *Power Action and Belief: A New Sociology of Knowledge,* ed. John Law. Sociological Review Monograph, no. 32: 196–223. London: Routledge, 1986.

Cappella, Joseph N., and Kathleen Hall Jamieson. *Spiral of cynicism: The press and the public good.* New York: Oxford University Press, 1997.

Carothers, Thomas. *Assessing democracy assistance: The case of Romania.* Washington, DC: Carnegie Endowment for International Peace, 1996.

Case, John, and Rosemary C.R. Taylor, eds. *Co-ops, communes and collectives: Experiments in social change in the 1960s and 1970s.* New York: Pantheon Books, 1979.

Cassen, Bernard. "Democracia participativa em Porto Alegre: Uma experiência exemplar no Brasil." *Jornal de olho no orçamento* (1998): 4.

Castells, Manuel. *The city and the grassroots.* London: Edward Arnold, 1983.

Castillo, Marco. "Reflections on participatory budgeting in New York City." *Innovation Journal: The Public Sector Innovation Journal* 20, no. 2 (2015).

Castoriadis, Cornelius. *The imaginary institution of society.* Cambridge, MA: MIT Press, 1998.

———. *La montée de l'insignifiance: Les Carrefours du Labyrinthe 4.* Paris: Seuil, 1996.

———. *La societé bureaucratique.* Paris: Christian Bourgois, 1990.

———. "Radical imagination and the social instituting imaginary." In *Rethinking imagination: Culture and creativity,* ed. G. Robinson and J. Rundell. London: Routledge, 1994.

———. *Une société à la dérive: Entretiens et débats, 1974–1997.* Paris: Seuil, 2005.

Cha, Ariana Eunjung. "Vallejo, Calif., once bankrupt, is now a model for cities in an age of austerity." *Washington Post,* May 23, 2012. www.washingtonpost. com/business/economy/vallejo-calif-once-bankrupt-is-now-a-model-for-cities-in-an-age-of-austerity/2012/05/23/gJQAjLKglU_story.html

Chaloupka, William. *Everybody knows: Cynicism in America.* Minneapolis: University of Minnesota Press, 1999.

Chambers, Robert. *Rural development: Putting the last first.* London: Longman, 1983.

Clark, Charles. "Reinventing government—Two decades later." *Government Executive,* April 26, 2013. Accessed December 4, 2014. www.govexec.com/management/2013/04/what-reinvention-wrought/62836/

Cleaver, Frances. "Paradoxes of participation: Questioning participatory approaches to development." *Journal of International Development* 11, no. 4 (1999): 597–612.

Cohen, Jean L., and Andrew Arato. *Civil society and political theory.* Cambridge, MA: MIT Press, 1992.

Cohen, Joshua. "Deliberation and democratic legitimacy." In *Deliberative democracy,* ed. J. Bohman and W. Rehg, 67–92. Cambridge, MA: MIT Press, 1997.

———. "Politics, power, and public reason." Tanner Lectures on Human Values, University of California, Berkeley, April 11, 2007.

Cohen, Joshua, and Joel Rogers. "Associations and democracy." *Social Philosophy and Policy* 10, no. 2 (1993): 282–312.

———. "Power and reason." In *Deepening democracy: Institutional innovations in empowered participatory governance,* ed. Archon Fung and Erik Olin Wright, 237–55. London/New York: Verso, 2003.

Colino, César, and Eloísa Del Pino. "Un fantasma recorre Europa: Renovación democrática mediante iniciativas de promoción participativa en los gobiernos locales." *II Jornadas de Sociología Política. Comunicación. Madrid: UNED (11–12 septiembre),* 2003.

Contreras-Becerra, J. "El movimiento vecinal en Andalucía durante el tardofranquismo y el proceso de cambio político (1968–1986): ¿Excepcionalidad o actor destacado?" *Revista Geronimo de Uztariz* 28 (2012): 95–122.

Cooke, Bill, and Uma Kothari, eds. *Participation: The new tyranny?* London: Zed Books, 2001.

Council of Europe, Committee of Ministers. "Participation of citizens in local public life." Recommendation Rec (2001) 19. Accessed September 10, 2006. www.coe.int

Craig, Stephen C. *The malevolent leaders: Popular discontent in America.* Boulder, CO: Westview Press, 1993.

Cratz, R. *The battle for Gotham: New York in the shadow of Robert Moses and Jane Jacobs.* New York: Nation Books, 2011.

Crenson, Matthew A., and Benjamin Ginsberg. *Downsizing democracy: How America sidelined its citizens and privatized its public*. Baltimore: Johns Hopkins University Press, 2004.

Crouch, Colin. *Post-democracy*. Cambridge: Polity, 2004.

Crozier, M., S. P. Huntington, and J. Watanuki. *The crisis of democracy*. New York: New York University Press, 1975.

Curtis, Jennifer. "'Profoundly ungrateful': The paradoxes of Thatcherism in Northern Ireland." *PoLAR: Political and Legal Anthropology Review* 33, no. 2 (2010): 201–24.

Dahl, A., and J. Soss. "Neoliberalism for the common good? Public value governance and the downsizing of democracy." *Public Administration Review* 74, no. 4 (2014): 496–504.

Dalton, Russell J. *Democratic challenges, democratic choices: The erosion of political support in advanced industrial democracies*. Oxford: Oxford University Press, 2007.

Davidson, Mark, and William Kutz. "Grassroots austerity: Municipal bankruptcy from below in Vallejo, California." *Environment and Planning A* 47, no. 7 (2015): 1440–59.

Denhardt, J. V., and R. B. Denhardt. "The new public service revisited." *Public Administration Review, On-line* (October 2015): 1–9.

Denhardt, Robert B., and Janet Vinzant Denhardt. "The new public service: Serving rather than steering." *Public Administration Review* 60, no. 6 (2000): 549–59.

Dewey, John. *The public and its problems: An essay in political inquiry*. Athens: Ohio University Press, 1954.

Dezalay, Yves, and Bryant G. Garth. *The internationalization of palace wars: Lawyers, economists, and the contest to transform Latin American states*. Chicago: University of Chicago Press, 2002.

Dios Mellado, Juan de, and Pablo Juliá. *Memoria de la transición democrática en Córdoba*. Seville: Centro de Estudios Andaluces, 2005.

Downey, Gary L. "Ideology and the clamshell identity: Organizational dilemmas in the anti-nuclear power movement." *Social Problems* (1986): 357–73.

Dunleavy, Patrick, and Christopher Hood. "From old public administration to new public management." *Public Money and Management* 14, no. 3 (1994): 916.

Dunleavy, Patrick, Helen Margetts, Simon Bastow, and Jane Tinkler. "New public management is dead: Long live digital-era governance." *Journal of Public Administration Research and Theory* 16, no. 3 (2006): 467–94.

Eggers, William. *Government 2.0: Using technology to improve education, cut red tape, reduce gridlock, and enhance democracy*. New York: Rowman & Littlefield, 2005.

Eliasoph, Nina. *Avoiding politics: How Americans produce apathy in everyday life*. Cambridge: Cambridge University Press, 1998.

Epstein, Barbara. *Political protest and cultural revolution: Nonviolent direct action in the 1970s and 1980s.* Berkeley: University of California Press, 1991.

Evans, Peter. "Counterhegemonic globalization: Transnational social movements in the contemporary global economy." In *The handbook of political sociology*, ed. T. Janoski, R. R. Alford, and A. M. Hicks, 1. Cambridge: Cambridge University Press, 2005.

Fattore, Giovanni, Hans F.W. Dubois, and Antonio Lapenta. "Measuring new public management and governance in political debate." *Public Administration Review* 72, no. 2 (2012): 218–27.

Fedozzi, Luciano. *Orçamento participativo: Reflexões sobre a experiência de Porto Alegre.* Porto Alegre: Tomo Editorial, 2001.

Ferguson, Daniel. "Understanding horizontal governance." Quebec: Centre for Literacy of Quebec, 2009.

Ferguson, James. *The anti-politics machine: "Development," depoliticization, and bureaucratic power in Lesotho.* Cambridge University Press Archive, 1990.

———. *Give a man a fish: Reflections on the new politics of distribution.* Durham, NC: Duke University Press, 2015.

———. "The uses of neoliberalism." *Antipode* 41 (2010): 171.

Font, Joan. *Ciudadanos y decisiones públicas.* Ariel, 2001.

Font, Joan, Donatella Della Porta, and Yves Sintomer. *Participatory democracy in Southern Europe: Causes, characteristics and consequences.* London: Rowman & Littlefield International, 2014.

Fórum Nacional de Participação Popular (FNPP). *Experiências de orçamento participativo no Brasil: Período de 1997 a 2000.* Petrópolis: Vozes, 2003.

Francis, Paul, Bill Cooke, and Uma Kothari. "Participatory development at the World Bank: The primacy of process." In *Participation: The new tyranny?* ed. Bill Coke and Uma Kothari, 72–87. London: Zed Books, 2001.

Fraser, Nancy. "Rethinking the public sphere: A contribution to the critique of actually existing democracy." In *Habermas and the public sphere*, ed. Craig Calhoun, 109–43. Cambridge, MA: MIT Press, 1992.

Fung, Archon. "Putting the public back into governance: The challenges of citizen participation and its future." *Public Administration Review* 75, no. 4 (2015): 513–22.

Fung, Archon, and Erik Olin Wright, eds. *Deepening democracy: Institutional innovations in empowered participatory governance.* London/New York: Verso, 2003.

Gallon, Michel. "Some elements of a sociology of translation." In *The science studies reader*, ed. Mario Biagioli, 67. London: Routledge, 1999.

Ganuza, Ernesto. "Les origines des budgets participatif." In *La démocratie participative inachevée*, ed. Marie-Hélène Bacque and Yves Sintomer, 23–42. Paris: Adels et Yves Michel, 2010.

Ganuza, Ernesto, and Francisco Francés. "The deliberative turn in participation: The problem of inclusion and deliberative opportunities in participatory budgeting." *European Political Science Review* 4, no. 2 (2012): 283–302.

———. *El círculo virtuoso de la democracia: Los presupuestos participativos a debate.* Madrid: CIS, 2012.

———. "Le défi participatif: Délibération et inclusion démocratique dans les budgets participatifs." *Revue Participations* 1 (2015): 167–89.

Ganuza, Ernesto, Héloïse Nez, and Ernesto Morales. "The struggle for a voice: Tensions between associations and citizens in participatory budgeting." *International Journal of Urban and Regional Research* (2014): 2274–91.

García Fernández, J., and M. D. González Ruiz. *Presente y futuro de las asociaciones de vecinos.* Madrid: Precosa Editorial, 1976.

García, Soledad. "Urban communities and local political participation in Spain." *Annals of the American Academy of Political and Social Science* (1995): 63–76.

Geissel, Brigitte. "Impact of democratic innovations in Europe: Findings and desiderata." In *Evaluating democratic innovations: Curing the democratic malaise?* ed. Brigitte Geissel and Kenneth Newton, 163–83. London: Routledge, 2012.

Genro, Tarso. "Licoes da intervencao." In *A intervencao nos transportes coletivos,* ed. J. A. d. Lima, 58. 1990.

Genro, Tarso, and Ubiratan de Souza. *Orcamento participativo: A experiencia de Porto Alegre.* São Paulo, 1997.

Gibson, Lima, and E. Luzzatto. "Entrevista: Administraqao popular em Porto Alegre: Dilemas e desafios." In *Uma aventura responsavel: Novos desafios das administracoes populares,* 80. 1993.

Gilman, Hollie. "Innovation is not just apps." Brookings. November 4, 2014. www.brookings.edu/blogs/techtank/posts/2014/11/4-innovation-apps

Ginzburg, Carlo. *Clues, myths, and the historical method.* Baltimore: Johns Hopkins University Press, 2013.

Gittell, Marilyn, et al. *Limits to citizen participation: The decline of community organizations.* Beverly Hills, CA: Sage, 1980.

Godwin, M. L. "Civic engagement and fiscal stress in American cities: Insights from the great recession." *State and Local Government Review* 46, no. 4 (2014): 249–59.

Goldfarb, Jeffrey C. *The cynical society: The culture of politics and the politics of culture in American life.* Chicago: University of Chicago Press, 1991.

Goldfrank, Benjamin. "The World Bank and the globalization of participatory budgeting." *Journal of Public Deliberation* 8, no. 2 (2012): 7.

Goldsmith, Arthur A. "Is governance reform a catalyst for development?" *Governance* 20, no. 2 (2007): 165–86.

Grazia, Grazia de, and Ana Clara de Torres Ribeiro. *Orçamento participativo no Brasil.* Editora Vozes, 2002.

Guerrero, M. *Veinte años de encuentros y desencuentros de las asociaciones de vecinos.* Madrid: Confederación de Asociaciones de Vecinos de España, 1998.

Gutmann, Amy, and Dennis Thompson. *Why deliberative democracy?* Princeton, NJ: Princeton University Press, 2009.

Habermas, Jürgen. *Between facts and norms.* Cambridge: Polity Press, 1996.

———. *Between naturalism and religion.* Cambridge: Polity Press, 2008.

———. *The theory of communicative action.* Vol. 2. Boston: Beacon Press, 1989.

Harnecker, Mara. *Brasil, la alcaldía de Porto Alegre: Aprendiendo a gobernar.* Colección: Haciendo camino al andar, no. 2. Cuba: Ediciones MEPLA, 1993.

Harvey, David. *A brief history of neoliberalism.* Oxford: Oxford University Press, 2005.

———. *The urban experience.* Baltimore: Johns Hopkins University Press, 1989.

Hay, Colin. *Why we hate politics.* Cambridge: Polity Press, 2011.

He, Baogan. "Civic engagement through participatory budgeting in China: Three different logics at work." *Public Administration and Development* 31 (2011): 122–31.

Held, David. *Prospects for democracy: North, south, east, west.* Stanford, CA: Stanford University Press, 1993.

Hendriks, Carolyn. "Institutions of deliberative democratic processes and interest groups: Roles, tensions and incentives." *Australian Journal of Public Administration* 61, no. 1 (2002): 64–75.

Herbert-Cheshire, Lynda, and Vaughan Higgins. "From risky to responsible: Expert knowledge and the governing of community-led rural development." *Journal of Rural Studies* 20, no. 3 (2004): 289–302.

Hetland, Gabriel. "The crooked line: From populist mobilization to participatory democracy in Chávez-era Venezuela." *Qualitative Sociology* 37, no. 4 (2014): 373-401.

Hickey, Samuel, and Giles Mohan, eds. *Participation—From tyranny to transformation? Exploring new approaches to participation in development.* London: Zed Books, 2004.

Hood, Christopher. "A public management for all seasons?" *Public Administration* 69, no. 1 (1991): 3–19.

Inglehart, Ronald. *Culture shift in advanced industrial society.* Princeton, NJ: Princeton University Press, 1990.

———. *Modernization and postmodernization: Cultural, economic, and political change in 43 societies.* Princeton, NJ: Princeton University Press, 1997.

———. "The renaissance of political culture." *American Political Science Review* 82, no. 4 (1988): 1203–30.

Jabola-Carolus, Isaac. "Injecting democracy into public spending." Occupy .com. April 15, 2013. www.occupy.com/article/injecting-democracy-public -spending

Jacobi, Pedro. "Movimentos sociais: Teoria e pratica em questao." In *Uma revolucao no cotidiano? Os novos movimentos sociais na America Latina*, ed. Ilse Scherer-Warren and Paulo Krische, 246–75. São Paulo: Brasiliense, 1987.

———. *Politicas sociais e ampliação da cidadania*. Rio de Janeiro: Fundação Getúlio Vargas, 2000.

Jasanoff, Sheila. *The fifth branch: Science advisers as policymakers*. Cambridge, MA: Harvard University Press, 1990.

Jordan, Grant, and William A. Maloney. *The protest business? Mobilising campaign groups*. Manchester: Manchester University Press, 1997.

Kaplan, Thomas. "Coalition seeks public's advice on New York City's goals." *New York Times*, November 6, 2013. Accessed December 1, 2014.

Kasdan, A., E. Markman, and P. Covey. "A People's Budget: A research and evaluation report on the participatory budgeting in New York City in 2013–2014." Tentative title; forthcoming.

Katinas, Paula. "Menchaca's goal: 'I want to be part of a movement.'" *Brooklyn Daily Eagle*, September 17, 2015. www.brooklyneagle.com/articles/2015/9/17/menchaca%E2%80%99s-goal-%E2%80%98i-want-be-part-movement%E2%80%99

Keane, John. *The life and death of democracy*. New York: Simon & Schuster, 2009.

Kębłowski, Wojciech, and Mathieu Van Criekingen. "How 'alternative' alternative urban policies really are?" *Métropoles* 15 (2014). Accessed February 24, 2015. metropoles.revues.org/4994

Keck, Margaret E., and Kathryn Sikkink. *Activists beyond borders: Advocacy networks in international politics*. Ithaca, NY: Cornell University Press, 1998.

Kersting, Norbert, and Angelika Vetter. *Reforming local government in Europe*. Frankfurt: VS Verlag, 2003.

Kleine, A., and M. Von Hauff. "Sustainability-driven implementation of corporate social responsibility: Application of the integrative sustainability triangle." *Journal of Business Ethics* 85, Suppl. 3 (2009): 517–33.

Klingemann, Hans-Dieter, and Dieter Fuchs, eds. *Citizens and the state*. Oxford: Oxford University Press, 1995.

Kothari, Uma. "Power, knowledge and social control in participatory development." In *Participation: The new tyranny*, ed. Bill Cooke and Uma Kothari, 139-52. London: Zed Books, 2001.

Laclau, Ernesto. *On populist reason*. London: Verso, 2005.

Laclau, Ernesto, and Chantal Mouffe. *Hegemony and socialist strategy: Towards a radical democratic politics*. London: Verso, 2001.

Laird, Lance D., and Wendy Cadge. "Negotiating ambivalence: The social power of Muslim community-based health organizations in America." *PoLAR: Political and Legal Anthropology Review* 33, no. 2 (2010): 225–44.

Landemore, Hélène. "Deliberation, cognitive diversity, and democratic inclusiveness: An epistemic argument for the random selection of representatives." *Synthese* 190, no. 7 (2013): 1209–31.

Lang, Amy. "Citizen learning in state-sponsored institutions: Accounting for variation in the British Columbia and Ontario citizens' assemblies on electoral reform." In *Learning citizenship by practicing democracy: International initiatives and perspectives*, ed. E. Pinnington and D. Schugurensky. Newcastle: Cambridge Scholars, 2010.

Lasch, Christopher. "The politics of nostalgia." *Harper's* 269 (1984): 65–70.

———. *The revolt of the elites and the betrayal of democracy*. New York: Norton, 1996.

Lascoumes, Pierre, and Patrick Le Gales. "Introduction: Understanding public policy through its instruments—From the nature of instruments to the sociology of public policy instrumentation." *Governance* 20, no. 1 (2007): 1–21.

Latour, Bruno. *Science in action: How to follow scientists and engineers through society*. Cambridge, MA: Harvard University Press, 1987.

Law, John, and Annemarie Mol. "Situating technoscience: An inquiry into spatialities." *Environment and Planning D: Society and Space* 19 (2001): 609–21.

Leachman, Mike, Phil Nyden, Bill Peterman, and Darnell Coleman. *Black, white, and shades of brown: Fair housing and economic opportunity in the Chicago region*. Chicago: Leadership Council for Metropolitan Open Communities, 1998.

Leal, Pablo. "Participation: The ascendancy of a buzzword in the neo-liberal era." *Development in Practice* 17, nos. 4–5 (2007): 539–48.

Lee, Caroline W. *Do-it-yourself democracy: The rise of the public engagement industry*. Oxford: Oxford University Press, 2015.

Lee, Caroline W., Michael McQuarrie, and Edward T. Walker, eds. *Democratizing inequalities: Dilemmas of the new public participation*. New York: New York University Press, 2015.

Legrán, Francisco. *El movimiento ciudadano Andaluz en la democracia*. Seville: Copistería Sevillana, 1977.

Leighninger, Matthew. *The next form of democracy: How expert rule is giving way to shared governance—And why politics will never be the same*. Nashville, TN: Vanderbilt University Press, 2006.

Lerner, J. *Everyone counts: Could "participatory budgeting" change democracy?* Ithaca, NY: Cornell University Press, 2014.

Leubolt, Bernhard, Andreas Novy, and Joachim Becker. "Changing patterns of participation in Porto Alegre." *International Social Science Journal* 59, nos. 193–94 (2008): 435–48.

Li, Tania Murray. "Beyond 'the state' and failed schemes." *American Anthropologist* 107, no. 3 (2005): 383–94.

Lichterman, Paul. "Seeing structure happen: Theory-driven participant observation." *Methods of social movement research* (2002): 118–45.

Lima, Gildo. "A experiencia da prefeitura de Porto Alegre." In *Prefeituras do povo e para o povo*, ed. I. Lesbaupin. São Paulo: Edições Loyola, 1996.

Lima, Gilson. *Uma aventura responsavel: Novos desafios das administrações populares.* Sagra-DC Luzzatto, 1993.

Lima Figueiredo, José Rubens de, Jr., and Bolivar Lamounier. *As cidades que dão certo: Experiências inovadoras na administração pública brasileira.* Vol. 1. Mh Comunicacao, 1997.

Lowndes, Vivien, Lawrence Pratchett, and Gerry Stoker. "Trends in public participation: Part 1—Local government perspectives." *Public Administration* 79, no. 1 (2001): 205–22.

Luce, Stephanie. "Lessons from living wage campaigns." *Works and Occupations* 32, no. 4 (2005): 423–40.

Madsen, Richard, William M. Sullivan, Ann Swidler, and Steven M. Tipton. *Individualism and commitment in American life: Readings on the themes of habits of the heart.* San Francisco: Harper & Row, 1987.

Magnier, Annick. "Between institutional learning and re-legitimization: Italian mayors in the unending reform." *International Journal of Urban and Regional Research* 28, no. 1 (2004): 166–82.

Maloney, William A., and Sigrid Rossteutscher, eds. *Social capital and associations in European democracies: A comparative analysis.* London: Routledge, 2007.

Maly, Michael, and Michael Leachman. "Rogers Park, Edgewater, Uptown, and Chicago Lawn, Chicago." *Cityscape* 4, no. 2 (1999).

Manin, Bernard, Elly Stein, and Jane Mansbridge. "On legitimacy and political deliberation." *Political Theory* 15, no. 3 (1987): 338–68.

Mansuri, Ghazala, and Vijayendra Rao. *Localizing development: Does participation work?* Washington, DC: World Bank, 2013.

Marx, Vanessa. *Las ciudades internacionales: Las ciudades como actors politicos en las relaciones internacionales.* Saarbrucken: VDM Verlag, 2010.

Mayr, Ernst. "When is historiography Whiggish?" *Journal of the History of Ideas* (1990): 301–9.

McQuarrie, Michael. "No contest: Participatory technologies and the transformation of urban authority." *Public Culture* 25, no. 1 (2013): 143–75.

Melo, Marcus Andre, and Gianpaolo Baiocchi. "Deliberative democracy and local governance: Towards a new agenda." *International Journal of Urban and Regional Research* 30, no. 3 (2006): 587–600.

Mendelberg, Tali. "The deliberative citizen: Theory and evidence." *Political Decision Making, Deliberation and Participation* 6, no. 1 (2002): 151–93.

Micheletti, Michele, and Dietlind Stolle, eds. *Politics, products, and markets: Exploring political consumerism past and present.* Piscataway, NJ: Transaction, 2004.

Milner, S. "Urban governance and local democracy in France." Political Studies Association, annual conference, April 2003. Accessed January 2012. www.psa.ac.uk/cps

Mohan, Giles. "Beyond participation: Strategies for deeper sovereignty." In *Participation: The new tyranny*, ed. Bill Cooke and Uma Kothari, 153–67. London: Zed Books, 2001.

Molotch, Harvey. *Managed integration: Dilemmas of doing good in the city.* Berkeley: University of California Press, 1972.

Montero, Sergio. 2009. "Experimenting with neoliberalism and democracy: The transformation of urban and regional governance in Bogotá, Colombia, in the context of decentralization." Master's thesis, University of California, Berkeley, 2009.

Mosse, David. "Anti-social anthropology? Objectivity, objection, and the ethnography of public policy and professional communities." *Journal of the Royal Anthropological Institute* 12, no. 4 (2006): 935–56.

Mouffe, Chantal. *The democratic paradox.* London: Verso, 2000.

———. *The return of the political.* London: Verso, 1993.

Murray, Kate M. "Regulating activism: An institutional ethnography of public participation." *Community Development Journal* (2011): bsr022.

Nam, Taewoo. "Suggesting frameworks of citizen-sourcing via government 2.0." *Government Information Quarterly* 29, no. 1 (2012): 12–20.

National League of Cities. *Making local democracy work: Municipal officials' views about public engagement.* Washington, DC: National League of Cities, 2010. Accessed December 1, 2014. www.nlc.org/documents/Find%20City%20Solutions/Research%20Innovation/Governance-Civic/making-local-democracy-work-rpt-10.pdf

———. "National municipal policy and resolutions." 2010. Accessed December 5, 2014. www.nlc.org/File%20Library/Influence%20Federal%20Policy/NMP/nlc-national-municipal-policy-book-2010.pdf

Navarro, Zander. "'Participatory budgeting'—The case of Porto Alegre (Brazil)." In *Regional workshop: Decentralization in Latin America—Innovations and policy implications.* Caracas, 1996.

Newton, Kenneth. "Curing the democratic malaise with democratic innovations." In *Evaluating democratic innovations: Curing the democratic malaise*, ed. Brigitte Geissel and Kenneth Newton, 3–20. London: Routledge, 2012.

———. "Institutional confidence and social trust." In *Political disaffection in contemporary democracies: Social capital, institutions, and politics*, 81–100. London: Routledge, 2006.

Nez, Héloïse, and Ernesto Ganuza. "Among militants and deliberative laboratories: The indignados." From Social to Political: New Forms of Mobilization and Democratization, international workshop, Universidad del País Vasco, Bilbao, 2012.

Norberto, Bobbio, "El tiempo de los derechos." *Sistema, España* (1991): 40.

Norris, Pippa. *Democratic deficit: Critical citizens revisited.* Cambridge: Cambridge University Press, 2011.

Norris, Pippa, Stefaan Walgrave, and Peter van Aelst. "Does protest signify disaffection? Demonstrators in a postindustrial democracy." In *Political disaffection in contemporary democracies: Social capital, institutions and politics,* 279–307. London: Routledge, 2006.

Nyden, Philip, Anne Figert, Mark Shibley, and Darryl Burrows. *Building community: Science in action.* Thousand Oaks, CA: Pine Forge Press, 1997.

Nyden, Philip, Michael Maly, and John Lukehart. "The emergence of stable racially and ethnically diverse urban communities: A case study of nine U.S. cities." *Housing Policy Debate* 8, no. 2 (1997): 491–534.

Nye, Joseph S., Philip Zelikow, and David C. King, eds. *Why people don't trust government.* Cambridge, MA: Harvard University Press, 1997.

NYT Editorial Board. "Leave an idea, take an idea." *New York Times*, November 22, 2013. Accessed December 1, 2014. www.nytimes.com/2013/11/23/opinion/leave-an-idea-take-an-idea.html?mabReward=relbias:r&adxnnl=1&module=Search&adxnnlx=1412107513-9joeE7jykn5K8bYAJEMfJA

Offe, Claus. "Governance: An 'empty signifier'?" *Constellations* 16, no. 4 (2009): 550–62.

———. "Social protection in a supranational context." *Globalization and Egalitarian Redistribution* (2006): 33.

Oliveira, Osmany Porto de. "Embaixadores da participação: A difusão internacional do Orçamento Participativo a partir do Brasil." Doctoral dissertation, University of São Paulo, 2013.

Ong, Aihwa. *Neoliberalism as exception: Mutations in citizenship and sovereignty.* Cambridge: Cambridge University Press, 2006.

Organisation for Economic Co-operation and Development. "Annual report 2003." Accessed December 1, 2014. www.oecd.org/about/2506789.pdf

———. *Citizens as partners.* 2000. Accessed December 2013.

———. "Governance in the 21st century." Future Studies series. 2001. Accessed December 4, 2014. www.oecd.org/futures/17394484.pdf

Osborne, David, and Ted Gaebler. "Reinventing government: How the entrepreneurial spirit is transforming the public sector." *Harvard Blackletter Journal* 9 (1992): 163.

O'Toole, J. B. *The ideal of public service: Reflections on the higher civil service in Britain.* London: Routledge, 2006.

Peck, Jamie. "Cities beyond compare?" *Regional Studies* 49, no. 1 (2015): 160–82.

Peck, Jamie, and Nik Theodore. *Fast policy: Experimental statecraft at the thresholds of neoliberalism.* Minneapolis: University of Minnesota Press, 2015.

———. "Mobilizing policy: Models, methods, and mutations." *Geoforum* 41, no. 2 (2010): 169–74.

Peck, Jamie, Nik Theodore, and Neil Brenner. "Postneoliberalism and its malcontents." *Antipode* 41 (2009): 94–116.

Pharr, Susan, and Robert Putnam, eds. *Disaffected democracies: What's troubling the trilateral countries.* Princeton, NJ: Princeton University Press, 2000.

Pharr, Susan, Robert Putnam, and Russell Dalton. "A quarter-century of declining confidence." *Journal of Democracy* 11, no. 2 (2000): 5–25.

Pinçon, Michel, and Monique Pinçon-Charlot. "Sociologia da alta burguesia." *Sociologias* 18 (2007): 22–37.

Pitkin, Hanna Fenichel. *The concept of representation.* Berkeley: University of California Press, 1967.

Pleyers, G. *Alter-globalization: Becoming actors in the Global Age.* Cambridge: Polity Press, 2010.

Polletta, Francesca. "Awkward movements." Special section edited by Polletta in *Mobilization* 11, no. 4 (2006): 475–78.

———. "How participatory democracy became white: Culture and organizational choice." *Mobilization: An International Quarterly* 10, no. 2 (2005): 271–88.

———. "Is participation without power good enough? Introduction to 'Democracy Now: Ethnographies of Contemporary Participation.'" *Sociological Quarterly* 55, no. 3 (2014): 453–66.

———. "Participatory democracy in the new millennium." *Contemporary Sociology* 42, no. 1 (2013): 40–50.

———. "Social movement cultures." In *The sociology of culture: A handbook,* ed. Laura Grindstaff, John Hall, and Ming-Chen Lo. London: Routledge, 2010.

Pont, Raul. *Democracia, igualdade e qualidade de vida: A experiencia de Porto Alegre.* Porto Alegre: Veraz Editora, 2003.

———. "Porto Alegre e a luta pela democracia, igualdade e qualidade de vida." *Porto Alegre: Uma cidade que conquista. A terceira gestão do PT no Governo Municipal, Porto Alegre: Artes e Ofícios,* 2000.

Porto Alegre. "Sobre o processo de discussão do orçamento." Representantes de Micro Regioes de Porto Alegre, FASE, 1989.

Prefeitura Municipal de Porto Alegre. "Conselho Municipal do Plano de Governo e Orçamento." Photocopy. 1990.

———. "Proceso de avaliaçao da gestao da Frente Popular." Gabinete do Prefeito, Coordenaçao de Relacoes com a Comunidades. Photocopy. 1992.

Preston, A., D. J. Cooper, and R. W. Coombs. "Fabricating budgets: A study of the production of management budgeting in the national health service." *Accounting, Organizations and Society* 17, no. 6 (1992): 561–93.

Przeworski, Adam. *Democracy and the limits of self-government.* New York: Cambridge University Press, 2010.

Purcell, Mark. "Urban democracy and the local trap." *Urban Studies* 43, no. 11 (2006): 1921–41.

————. *The down-deep delight of democracy.* Hoboken, NJ: Wiley, 2013.

Purdy, Jedediah. "After apathy." *American Prospect* 11, no. 2 (1999): 12–13.

Ramonet, Ignacio. "The promise of Porto Alegre, Le Monde Diplomatique." 2001. www.globalpolicy.org/socecon/tncs/davos/01pal1.htm

Rancière, Jacques. *Aux bords du politique.* Paris: Gallimard, Folio-Essais, 1998.

————. *The future of the image.* London: Verso, 2007.

————. *La haine de la démocratie.* Paris: La fabrique éditions, 2005.

————. "Ten theses on politics." *Theory and Event* 5, no. 3 (2001). Accessed September 2014. https://muse.jhu.edu/journals/theory_and_event/v005/5.3ranciere.html

Ratner, Lizzy. "New Yorkers are holding a great participatory policy-making conference: Will de Blasio listen?" *The Nation,* December 9, 2013. Accessed December 1, 2014. www.thenation.com/article/177294/new-yorkers-are-holding-great-participatory-policy-making-conference-will-de-blasio-l#

Rawls, John. "The idea of public reason revisited." *University of Chicago Law Review* 64 (1997): 809–30.

Ribeiro, Ana Clara Torres, and Grazia de Grazia. *Experiências de orçamento participativo no Brasil: Período de 1997 a 2000.* Fórum Nacional de Participação Popular, 2003.

Right to the City Alliance. "Right to the City charter." Accessed November 1, 2011. www.righttothecity.org

Roberts, Nancy. "Public deliberation in an age of direct citizen participation." *American Review of Public Administration* 34, no. 4 (2004): 315–53.

Robinson, Gillian, and John F. Rundell, eds. *Rethinking imagination: Culture and creativity.* Abingdon: Psychology Press, 1994.

Rosa, A., coord. *La estación de Córdoba: Historia de una lucha ciudadana.* Córdoba: Federación de Asociaciones de Vecinos Al-Zahara, 1995.

Rosanvallon, Pierre. *Democratic legitimacy: Impartiality, reflexivity, proximity.* Princeton, NJ: Princeton University Press, 2011.

Rose, Nikolas. "The death of the social? Re-figuring the territory of government." *International Journal of Human Resource Management* 25, no. 3 (1996): 327–56.

Roussopoulos, Dimitrios, and C. George Benello. *Participatory democracy: Prospects for democratizing democracy.* Montreal: Black Rose Books, 2005.

Ruiz, B. M. *Por un modelo público de agua: Triunfos, luchas y sueños*. Madrid: El Viejo Topo Editorial, 2005.

Sanders, Lynn M. "Against deliberation." *Political Theory* 25, no. 3 (1997): 347–76.

Santos, Boaventura de Sousa. *Democracia e participação: O caso do orçamento participativo de Porto Alegre*. Porto Alegre: Afrontamento, 2002.

Sartori, Giovanni, ed. *Social science concepts: A systematic analysis*. Beverly Hills, CA: Sage, 1984.

Saward, Michael. "Enacting democracy." *Political Studies* 51, no. 1 (2003): 161–79.

———. "Making democratic connections: Political equality, deliberation and direct democracy." *Acta Politica* 36, no. 4 (2001): 361–79.

Schumpeter, Joseph A. *Capitalism, socialism and democracy*. London: Routledge, 2013.

Scott, David. *Conscripts of modernity: The tragedy of colonial enlightenment*. Durham, NC: Duke University Press, 2004.

Scott, James C. *Domination and the arts of resistance: Hidden transcripts*. New Haven, CT: Yale University Press, 1990.

———. "The infrapolitics of subordinate groups." In *The Global Resistance Reader*, ed. Louise Amoore. London: Routledge, 2005.

Sheppard, Eric, and Helga Leitner. "*Quo vadis* neoliberalism? The remaking of global capitalist governance after the Washington Consensus." *Geoforum* 41, no. 2 (2010): 185–94.

Sintomer, Yves. *Petite histoire de l'expérimentation démocratique: Tirage au sort et politique d'Athènes à nos jours*. Paris: Broché, 2011.

Sintomer, Yves, and Jacques De Maillard. "The limits to local participation and deliberation in the French 'politique de la ville.'" *European Journal of Political Research* 46, no. 4 (2007): 503–29.

Sintomer, Yves, Carsten Herzberg, and Giovanni Allegretti. *Learning from the South: Participatory budgeting worldwide—An initiation to global cooperation: Study*. Bonn: Service Agency Communities in One World, 2010.

Sintomer, Yves, Carsten Herzberg, and Anja Röcke. "Démocratie participative et modernisation des services publics: Les affinités électives." In *Les budgets participatifs en Europe*. Paris: La Découverte, 2008.

Sirianni, Carmen, and Lewis Friedland. *Civic innovation in America: Community empowerment, public policy, and the movement for civic renewal*. Berkeley: University of California Press, 2001.

Skocpol, Theda. *Diminished democracy: From membership to management in American civic life*. Norman: University of Oklahoma Press, 2013.

———. "Voice and inequality: The transformation of American civic democracy." *Perspectives on Politics* 2, no. 1 (2004): 3–20.

Smith, Chris. "Q&A: The man behind the talking transition 'think tent' spills his secrets." *Daily Intelligencer*, November 22, 2013. Accessed December 1,

2014. http://nymag.com/daily/intelligencer/2013/11/man-behind-the-think -tent-tells-all.html

———. "Talking transition survey tells de Blasio's tale of two cities." *Daily Intelligencer,* February 10, 2014. Accessed December 2, 2014. http://nymag. com/daily/intelligencer/2014/02/survey-tells-de-blasios-tale-of-two-cities .html

Smith, Graham. *Democratic innovations: Designing institutions for citizen participation.* Cambridge: Cambridge University Press, 2009.

———. "Revitalising politics through democratic innovation?" *Representation* 45, no. 3 (2009).

Stewart, LaShonda M., Steven A. Miller, R. W. Hildreth, and Maja V. Wright-Phillips. "Participatory budgeting in the United States: A preliminary analysis of Chicago's 49th Ward experiment." *New Political Science* 36, no. 2 (2014): 193–218.

Stivers, Richard. *The culture of cynicism: American morality in decline.* Oxford: Blackwell, 1994.

Stoker, Gerry. "Public value management: A new narrative for networked governance?" *American Review of Public Administration* 36, no. 1 (2006): 41–57.

Strange, Susan, and Roger Tooze, eds. *The international politics of surplus capacity (Routledge Revivals): Competition for market shares in the world recession.* London: Routledge, 2010.

Su, Celina. "Between bottom-up and top-down governance: Participatory budgeting in New York City." *Metropolitics,* December 1, 2014. Accessed March 1, 2015. www.metropolitiques.eu/Participatory-Budgeting-in-New.html

———. "Whose budget? Our budget? Broadening political stakeholdership via participatory budgeting." *Journal of Public Deliberation* 2 (2012): 1–14.

Swyngedouw, Erik. "Governance innovation and the citizen: The Janus face of governance-beyond-the-state." *Urban Studies* 42, no. 11 (2005): 1991–2006.

———. "Impossible sustainability and the post-political condition." In *The sustainable development paradox: Urban political economy in the United States and Europe,* ed. Rob J. Krueger and David Gibbs, 13–40. New York: Guilford, 2007.

———. "Interrogating post-democratization: Reclaiming egalitarian political spaces." *Political Geography* 30 (2011): 370–80.

Talpin, Julien. *Schools of democracy: How ordinary citizens (sometimes) become competent in participatory budgeting institutions.* Colchester: ECPR Press, 2011.

Tenants and Workers United. "Projects." Accessed November 17, 2014. www. tenantsandworkers.org/our-projects/

Thompson, Andrew. "The battle for Necropolis." In *Urban commons: Moving beyond state and market,* ed. Mary Dellenbaugh, Martin Schwegmann, and Markus Kip, 214–35. Basel: Birkhäuser Verlag AG, 2015.

Thompson, Dennis F. "Deliberative democratic theory and empirical political science." *Annual Review of Political Science* 11 (2008): 497–520.

Thompson, James R. "Reinvention as reform: Assessing the National Performance Review." *Public Administration Review* 60, no. 6 (2000): 508–21.

Tocqueville, Alexis de. *Democracy in America: And two essays on America.* 1840. New York: Penguin Classics, 2003.

Tolchin, Susan J. *The angry American: How voter rage is changing the nation.* Boulder, CO: Westview Press, 1996.

Tormey, Simon. *The end of representative politics.* Cambridge: Polity Press, 2015.

Travaline, Patricia. "Clinton tells marketers we live in a participation age #MKT-GNATION14." *Content Standard,* April 9, 2014. Accessed December 1, 2014. www.skyword.com/contentstandard/blog/hillary-clinton-tells-marketers -we-live-in-a-participation-age-mktgnation14/

UN-Habitat. "The Habitat agenda goals and principles, commitments and the global plan of action." Istanbul: UN-Habitat, 1996.

Uniao das Associaçoes de Moradores de Porto Alegre (UAMPA). "Conselhos minicipais: Como devem funcionar, o que devem deliberar." Photocopy. 1986.

Urbinati, Nadia. "Competing for liberty: The Republican critique of democracy." *American Political Science Review* 106, no. 3 (2012): 607–21.

———. *Democracy disfigured: Opinion, truth and the people.* Cambridge, MA: Harvard University Press, 2014.

Utzig, José Eduardo. "Notas sobre o governo do PT em Porto Alegre." *Novos Estudos CEBRAP* 45 (1996): 209–22.

Vannier, Christian N. "Audit culture and grassroots participation in rural Haitian development." *PoLAR: Political and Legal Anthropology Review* 33, no. 2 (2010): 282–305.

Verba, Sidney, Kay Lehman Schlozman, and Henry E. Brady. *Voice and equality: Civic voluntarism in American politics.* Cambridge, MA: Harvard University Press, 1995.

Vigoda, Eran, and Robert T. Golembiewski. "Citizenship behavior and the spirit of new managerialism: A theoretical framework and challenge for governance." *American Review of Public Administration* 31, no. 3 (2001): 273–95.

Villasante, Tomás R. *Las democracias participativas.* Madrid: Hoac, 1995.

———. *Los vecinos en la calle: Por una alternativa democrática a la ciudad de los monopolios.* Madrid: Ediciones de la Torre, 1976.

Walker, E. T. *Grassroots for hire: Public affairs consultants in American democracy.* Cambridge: Cambridge University Press, 2014.

———. "Privatizing participation: Civic change and the organizational dynamics of grassroots lobbying firms." *American Sociological Review* 74 (2009): 83–105.

Walker, E. T., and C. M. Rea. "The political mobilization of firms and industries." *Annual Review of Sociology* 40 (August 2014): 281–304.

Wallace, David. "The otherness of Castoriadis." *TOPIA: Canadian Journal of Cultural Studies* 3 (2000).

Wampler, Brian. "Can participatory institutions promote pluralism? Mobilizing low-income citizens in Brazil." *Studies in Comparative International Development* 41, no. 4 (2007): 57–78.

———. "Entering the state: Civil society activism and participatory governance in Brazil." *Political Studies* 60, no. 2 (2012): 341–62.

———. "A guide to participatory budgeting." In *Participatory budgeting*, ed. Anwar Shah, 21–54. Washington, DC: World Bank, 2007.

Wampler, Brian, and Leonardo Avritzer. "The spread of participatory democracy in Brazil: From radical democracy to participatory good government." *Journal of Latin American Urban Studies* (2005).

Wampler, Brian, and J. Hartz-Karp. "Participatory budgeting: Diffusion and outcomes across the world." *Journal of Public Deliberation* 8 (2012).

Wampler, Brian, and Stephanie McNulty. "Does participatory governance matter?" Boise State University, 2011. Accessed September 2013. www.wilsoncen ter.org/publication/does-participatory-governance-matter

Weber, Rachel, Thea Crum, and Eduardo Salinas. "The civics of community development: Participatory budgeting in Chicago." *Community Development* 46, no. 3 (2015): 261–78.

Wedeen, Lisa. *Ambiguities of domination.* Chicago: University of Chicago Press, 1999.

Wennerhag, Magnus. "Another modernity is possible? The global justice movement and the transformations of politics." *Distinktion: Scandinavian Journal of Social Theory* 11, no. 2 (2010): 25–49.

Weyland, Kurt. *Bounded rationality and policy diffusion: Social sector reform in Latin America.* Princeton, NJ: Princeton University Press, 2009.

Wolfowitz, Paul. "Good governance and development: A time for action." World Bank. Accessed April 11, 2006. http://web.worldbank.org/WBSITE/EXTERNAL/ EXTABOUTUS/ORGANIZATION/EXTOFFICEPRESIDENT/0, contentMDK

World Bank. *World Bank participation sourcebook.* Washington, DC: World Bank, 1996.

World Bank Staff. *World development report 1997: The state in a changing world.* Oxford: Oxford University Press, 1997.

———. *World development report 2003: Sustainable development in a dynamic world—Transforming institutions, growth, and quality of life.* Oxford: Oxford University Press, 2003.

Wright, Erik Olin. *Envisioning real utopias.* London: Verso, 2010.

Wuthnow, Robert. "The United States: Bridging the privileged and the marginalized?" In *Democracies in flux: The evolution of social capital in contemporary society*, ed. Robert D. Putnam. New York: Oxford University Press, 2002.

Young, Iris Marion. "Communication and the other: Beyond deliberative democracy." In *Democracy and difference: Contesting the boundaries of the political*, ed. Seyla Benhabib, 120–35. Princeton, NJ: Princeton University Press, 1996.

Documents

"Bill de Blasio: Mayoral candidate—Decide NYC." Decide NYC. Accessed December 2, 2014. www.decidenyc.com/election-candidate/bill-deblasio/

"Coalition seeks public's advice on New York City's goals." *New York Times*, November 7, 2013.

"Communiqué sur la Conférence Internationale sur la Participation Citoyenne et Budgets Participatifs en Afrique." Inici. June 12, 2013. Accessed December 1, 2014. www.oidp.net/?id=101&L=3&action=detall&OIDP_content_ID=246&language=FR

"Forum Mondial de la Démocratie." Forum Mondial de la Démocratie. 2013. Accessed November 30, 2014. www.coe.int/web/world-forum-democracy/home-2013

"How to end with New Public Management: New perspectives for public action." International Public Management Symposium. May 14, 2014. Accessed September 21, 2016. www.economie.gouv.fr/files/program_en_rigp_2014_.pdf

"Making local democracy work: Municipal officials' views about public engagement." Report of the National League of Cities. Washington, DC, 2010. Accessed September 21, 2016. www.nlc.org/documents/Find%20City%20Solutions/Research%20Innovation/Governance-Civic/making-local-democracy-work-rpt-10.pdf

"Making the case: Conservatives." The People's Budget (London). Accessed May 16, 2012. www.thepeoplesbudget.org.uk/makethecase/conservative

"Mayor de Blasio announces the launch of the national 'Cities for Citizenship' effort." Official Website of the City of New York. September 17, 2014. Accessed December 2, 2014. www1.nyc.gov/office-of-the-mayor/news/444-14/mayor-de-blasio-the-launch-the-national-cities-citizenship-effort-mayors

"Mayor-elect Bill de Blasio on talking transition." YouTube. November 22, 2013. Accessed December 1, 2014. www.youtube.com/watch?v=-hM6UDxuTkQ

"OIDP distinction, 'Best Practice in Citizen Participation.'" Inici. June 1, 2014. Accessed December 2, 2014. www.oidp.net/?id=62&L=2&action=detall&OIDP_content_ID=355&language=EN

"Port Huron Statement of the Students for a Democratic Society, 1962." Accessed January 1, 2014. www.h-net.org/~Hst306/Documents/Huron.html

"Talking transition." Open Society Foundations. November 9, 2013. Accessed December 1, 2014. www.opensocietyfoundations.org/events/talking-transition

"The Open Government Partnership Second Open Government National Action Plan for the United States of America." December 5, 2013. Accessed December 1, 2014. www.whitehouse.gov/sites/default/files/docs/us_national _action_plan_6p.pdf

"The United States releases its Second Open Government National Action Plan." The White House. Accessed November 30, 2014. www.whitehouse.gov/blog/2013/ 12/06/united-states-releases-its-second-open-government-national-action-plan

Index